WALKI

—

MALHAMDALE

HILLSIDE GUIDES - ACROSS NORTHERN ENGLAND

The Uplands of Britain - full colour hardback books
- THE HIGH PEAKS OF ENGLAND & WALES
- YORKSHIRE DALES, MOORS & FELLS

Hillwalking - Lake District
- LAKELAND FELLS - SOUTH
- LAKELAND FELLS - EAST
- LAKELAND FELLS - NORTH
- LAKELAND FELLS - WEST

Long Distance Walks
- COAST TO COAST WALK
- DALES WAY
- CUMBRIA WAY
- WESTMORLAND WAY
- FURNESS WAY
- LADY ANNE'S WAY
- BRONTE WAY
- CALDERDALE WAY
- PENDLE WAY
- CLEVELAND WAY
- NIDDERDALE WAY
- TRANS-PENNINE WAY

Circular Walks - Yorkshire Dales
- WHARFEDALE
- MALHAMDALE
- SWALEDALE
- NIDDERDALE
- THREE PEAKS
- WENSLEYDALE
- HOWGILL FELLS
- HARROGATE & WHARFE VALLEY
- RIPON & LOWER WENSLEYDALE

Circular Walks - Peak District
- NORTHERN PEAK
- CENTRAL PEAK
- EASTERN PEAK
- SOUTHERN PEAK
- WESTERN PEAK

Circular Walks - Lancashire/North West
- BOWLAND
- PENDLE & THE RIBBLE
- WEST PENNINE MOORS
- ARNSIDE & SILVERDALE

Circular Walks - North Pennines
- TEESDALE
- EDEN VALLEY
- ALSTON & ALLENDALE

Circular Walks - North York Moors/York area
- WESTERN MOORS
- SOUTHERN MOORS
- HOWARDIAN HILLS

Circular Walks - South Pennines
- ILKLEY MOOR
- BRONTE COUNTRY
- CALDERDALE
- SOUTHERN PENNINES

*Send for a detailed current catalogue and price list
and also visit www.hillsidepublications.co.uk*

WALKING COUNTRY

—

MALHAMDALE

Paul Hannon

—

Hillside

HILLSIDE
PUBLICATIONS
20 Wheathead Crescent
Keighley
West Yorkshire
BD22 6LX

First published 1986
Fully Revised (6th) edition 2008

© Paul Hannon 1986, 2008

ISBN 978-1-870141-86-4

.

Cover illustration: Malham Cove
Back cover: Gordale; Kirkby Malham; Flasby Fell
Page One: Malham Tarn
Page Three: Sundial, Kirkby Malham
(Paul Hannon/Hillslides Picture Library)

The sketch maps in this book are based upon
1947 Ordnance Survey One-Inch maps

Printed in Great Britain by
Carnmor Print
95-97 London Road
Preston
Lancashire
PR1 4BA

CONTENTS

INTRODUCTION..6

THE WALKS (mileage in brackets)

1   Malham Classic (4$\frac{1}{2}$).........................8
2   Kirkby Fell (6$\frac{1}{4}$)..............................10
3   The Dry Valley (5)..............................13
4   Aire Head Springs (3$\frac{3}{4}$)....................16
5   Weets Top (7$\frac{1}{2}$)..............................20
6   Fountains Fell (8$\frac{1}{2}$)........................24
7   Stockdale (9$\frac{1}{2}$)..............................28
8   Gordale Scar (6)..............................32
9   Darnbrook (8$\frac{1}{2}$)..............................36
10 Mastiles Lane (7)..............................39
11 Calton Moor (8$\frac{3}{4}$)..........................42
12 Kirkby Malham (4$\frac{3}{4}$)........................46
13 Bell Busk (5)..............................50
14 Otterburn Moor (5$\frac{3}{4}$)......................53
15 Langber Lane (4$\frac{3}{4}$)..........................56
16 Coniston Cold (6$\frac{1}{4}$)..........................59
17 Around Eshton (5$\frac{3}{4}$)........................62
18 East Marton (6$\frac{1}{2}$)............................66
19 Winterburn Valley (6$\frac{1}{4}$)....................70
20 Bordley (5$\frac{1}{2}$)..............................73
21 Rylstone Edges (6)..........................76
22 Flasby Fell (6)..............................80
23 Embsay Moor (6$\frac{3}{4}$)..........................85
24 Crookrise Crag (5$\frac{3}{4}$)......................90

WALK LOG..94
USEFUL ADDRESSES..............................95
INDEX..96

INTRODUCTION

Malhamdale is the southernmost valley of the Yorkshire Dales National Park, taking its name from the village for which all visitors make. Its river is the Aire, which unlike its neighbours which also rise high in the Dales, has but a brief existence in these tranquil pastures before heading into industrial Yorkshire. Fortunately its time here is well spent, and along with its tributaries presents a highly compact area that offers rich contrasts. The western half comprises the stunning limestone scenery based on Malham Cove and Gordale Scar, with Malham Tarn also at the heart. Downstream from Malham the valley becomes pastoral, with several villages nestling by the river down to Gargrave where the Leeds-Liverpool Canal offers further delights. East of the Aire witness a dramatic change to gritstone country, with rocky outcrops, bracken slopes and the extensive heather sweep of Barden Moor. The various becks flowing off the moors all meet the Aire by the market town of Skipton, some having emerged from attractive reservoirs.

Malham itself has an appeal rather different to that of most Dales villages in that the majority of visitors come to walk, even though for most it's simply a return to the Cove. The centre has much of interest, with attractive 17th and 18th century cottages. The Listers Arms dates from 1723 and bears the arms of the Lords Ribblesdale, while the Buck Inn and several cafes offer further refreshment. In monastic times Bolton Priory and Fountains Abbey shared much of the land hereabouts, and reminders of their granges are found in the names of two of Malham's bridges, Monk Bridge and Prior Moon's clapper bridge. Useful modern, purpose-built structures are the youth hostel and National Park Centre.

Access to the countryside

The majority of walks are on rights of way with no access restrictions. A handful make use of 'Right to Roam', and these are noted in their introduction. Existing access areas now largely fall within these swathes of Open Country, and on most days of the year you are free to walk responsibly over these wonderful landscapes. Of various restrictions two most notable are that dogs are banned from grouse moors; and also that areas can close for up to 28 days each year, subject to advance notice. The most likely times will be from the 'Glorious Twelfth', the start of the grouse shooting season in August, though weekends should largely be unaffected.

Further information can be obtained from the Countryside Agency (see page 95), and ideally from information centres. Availability of any public transport is mentioned in the introduction to each walk.

Using the guide
    Each self contained walk sees essential information followed by a route description and simple map. In between are notes and illustrations of features along the way. Snippets of information are placed in *italics* to ensure essential route description is easier to locate. The sketch maps identify the location of the routes rather than fine detail, and whilst the description should be sufficient to guide you around, an Ordnance Survey map is strongly recommended. To gain the most from a walk, the detail of the 1:25,000 scale Explorer map is unsurpassed. It also gives the option to vary walks as desired, giving an improved picture of your surroundings and the availability of linking paths. Just one map covers all the walks in this book: • *Explorer OL2 - Yorkshire Dales South/West*
Also useful for planning are Landranger maps 98, 103 and 104.

WALKING COUNTRY
MALHAMDALE

6 Malham Tarn
Water Sinks Gate   10 Street Gate
7 8 9
1 2 3 4 5 Malham
20 Boss Moor
Kirkby Malham   11 Calton   Cracoe
Long Preston   12 13 Airton   Hetton   21
Winterburn   Rylstone   22
15   Otterburn   19
14   Hellifield   Coniston Cold   Eastby O
B6265   Embsay   23
Gargrave   A65   A59   24
16 17 18   SKIPTON

14 *walks*
● *start points*
O *other villages*

1
MALHAM CLASSIC

START *Malham   Grid ref. SD 900626*

DISTANCE *4¹2 miles (7km)*

ORDNANCE SURVEY MAPS
1:50,000
Landranger 98 - Wensleydale & Upper Wharfedale
1:25,000
Explorer OL2 - Yorkshire Dales South/West

ACCESS *Start from the village centre. National Park car park. Served by bus from Skipton.*

The definitive Malham walk visiting its two great landmarks

From the car park head into the village, crossing the beck either by a footbridge by the forge, or by using the road bridge and doubling back to follow the beck downstream. The short lane ends at a gate from where a broad path heads across the fields. At a double kissing-gate the main path swings left to a barn, crosses to the left of the wall and continues as before. *The outer portals of Gordale await, but as yet reveal nothing of the grandeur to come: Malham Cove, however, shows itself back over the village.*

Gordale Beck is joined and followed upstream. On entering a delightful section of woodland, the charming waterfall of Janet's Foss will be reached all too soon. *Legend has it that Janet, local fairy queen, had a cave behind the falls. More certain is that this wood is a rich habitat for a wide variety of flora and fauna.* Here the path breaks off left to emerge onto the road to Gordale. Turn right for a short distance, crossing the beck to reach a gate on the left just before Gordale House. A well trodden path crosses the pasture to the unmistakable cliffs of Gordale Scar, which converge as you enter the forbidding confines.

This most awe-inspiring single feature of the Yorkshire Dales waits for you to turn the final corner before impressing you to the full. Once in its depths the grandeur of the overhanging cliffs can initially be too daunting to appreciate the waterfalls: the upper fall spills spectacularly through a circular hole in the rocks. The water is Gordale Beck, funneled from the moors to the valley. WALK 8 continues through the ravine onto those moors.

Return to the old bridge and leave the road by a kissing-gate. From the wall corner just above, a grassy path climbs the fieldside to another gate, then rise to one at the top corner. Here a firm path runs along to the left, staying with the wall beneath open country. At the end it slants up to run parallel with the Malham Tarn road, joining it at a kissing-gate.

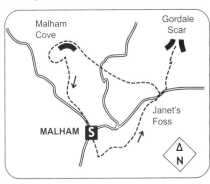

Cross straight over to a stile and a path heads across the pasture. A wall is joined and followed as far as the next corner. When the wall turns away, the route forks. While the right branch rises to a stile in the wall ahead, your way bears gently down to the left, with the limestone pavement at the top of Malham Cove revealed immediately below you. Drop down to a stile/gateway to access the top of the Cove. Up to the right, the Dry Valley strikes into the hills *(see WALK 3). The extensive pavement is fascinating to tread, but with care as the grikes in between have great leg-damaging capabilities. The limestone cliff of Malham Cove falls 300ft: imagine the waterfall that once plunged over here!*

At the far end a kissing-gate sends a stepped path descending the slopes at the end of the Cove. At the bottom, bear left to access the base of the mighty cliff. *Issuing from it is Malham Beck, having sunk on the moor.* To return to Malham turn downstream on a broad path through the fields to emerge onto the road just short of the village.

2

KIRKBY FELL

START *Malham*   *Grid ref. SD 900626*

DISTANCE *6^{1}4 miles (10km)*

ORDNANCE SURVEY MAPS
1:50,000
Landranger 98 - Wensleydale & Upper Wharfedale
1:25,000
Explorer OL2 - Yorkshire Dales South/West

ACCESS *Start from the village centre. National Park car park. Served by bus from Skipton. •OPEN ACCESS: see page 6.*

An absorbing limestone walk that briefly extends to gritstone: featuring big views and a good dose of historical interest

      From the car park entrance don't join the road into the village but turn up a walled track on the right, then right again almost immediately on a similar track. Ignore a grassy branch left opposite a barn and take the next track climbing to the left. On levelling out it forks, and your way is the main one, left. *Malham Cove is well seen across to the right, while Kirkby Fell and Pikedaw rise steeply ahead.* After a slab footbridge and ford leave the track by a stile on the right, and cross to a prominent barn, re-crossing the stream en-route. From the stile by it a path heads up the field, keeping above the beck to reach a stile/gateway at the top.

      Note the line of the Mid-Craven Fault along the course of the beck. The hills ahead also emphasise the marked transition from gritstone to limestone, as Kirkby Fell exhibits the former and Pikedaw the latter. Once height has been gained on leaving Malham, look back over the village to see, to particularly good advantage, the lynchets across the hillside. These are the ancient cultivation terraces of Anglian farmers, providing level strips to produce crops on steep slopes. The path maintains the same line, crossing the tiny stream to ascend pleasantly, passing an old spoil-heap before levelling out at a stile in the wall ahead. *Pikedaw Hill's crest is a short steep pull to the right, though most of its view can be savoured from your path: look back to see Barden Moor, Rombalds Moor, Flasby Fell and the South Pennines. Pikedaw is best known for its early 19th century mining activity. Chief target was calamine, a zinc ore, and evidence of this industry abounds in the form of shafts, levels and spoilheaps.*

From the stile resume straight up the slope in front (ignoring a lesser right fork), beneath limestone scars while looking across to the gritstone boulders on Kirkby Fell. After a short steeper pull the gradient eases and the path swings right up onto grassy moor-land. *Part way along is a first glimpse of the crouching lion of*

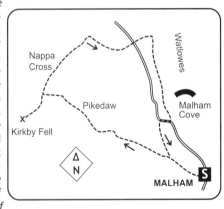

Penyghent through a gap ahead. The path ascends gently to the prominent Nappa Gate, passing pools and spoilheaps from calamine workings on the way. Just before merging with a broader bridle-track at the gate, a covered mineshaft is seen just to the right, by the track. Nappa Gate brings more features to the view, including Malham Tarn with Buckden Pike and Great Whernside beyond.

The next stage is a short detour to the summit of Kirkby Fell, returning to Nappa Gate. Through the gate take advantage of Open Access and turn left with the wall to a corner gate/stile. From here a faint quad track points the short distance up to Kirkby Fell's waiting summit. *Crowned by a scrappy cairn constructed from the scattered rocks, at 1791ft/546m this bleak hilltop is only marginally overtopped by neighbouring Rye Loaf Hill. The view, unsurprisingly, is an extensive if not intimate one, reaching out as much to Bowland and the Ribble Valley as into the Dales.*

Return to Nappa Gate and bear left on a grassy wallside path to the wall corner at Nappa Cross. *This is one of several way-side crosses in the area, a guidepost for travellers since monastic times. Set into the wall, the restored shaft stands in its original base. Ahead is a fine prospect of Malham Tarn in its upland bowl.* Beyond the cross, a delightful broad grassy way slopes down to a gate, and maintains this slant through further pastures to meet the similarly grassy Gorbeck Road at a corner. Turn right down this to descend to the road out of the village at Langscar Gate.

Cross straight over to a stile and a green path heads down the wallside: approaching a stile at the bottom, turn sharp right with a fence to reach a stile in the wall. The path runs a splendid course roughly parallel with the road up to the right, encountering several stiles in these limestone pastures. *Grand views look over the immediate limestone surrounds out to Weets Top, Cracoe Fell, Crookrise Crag, Flasby Fell, the Aire Valley and the South Pennines. Further, Malham village appears, along with old field boundaries and strip lynchets beneath the partly revealed Cove.*

Ultimately the path fades above a steeper slope: drop left to a stile in the wall below, and just beyond it a stile returns you to the road. *For a quicker finish turn down it into the village.* Turn uphill for a short distance to a sharp bend, and here take a gate on the left: a track heads down to a gate where it becomes enclosed by walls to lead pleasantly past an earlier junction. Continue to the T-junction below. To finish through the village, turn left here and almost immediately right down a walled path to emerge opposite Beck Hall. A right turn will then lead back to the start.

Nappa Cross

3

THE DRY VALLEY

START *Malham   Grid ref. SD 900626*

DISTANCE *5 miles (8km)*

ORDNANCE SURVEY MAPS
1:50,000
Landranger 98 - Wensleydale & Upper Wharfedale
1:25,000
Explorer OL2 - Yorkshire Dales South/West

ACCESS *Start from the village centre. National Park car park. Served by bus from Skipton.*

Very easy walking through stunning limestone scenery: a must!

From the car park pass through the village, keeping left at the junction by the bridge. After the cluster of buildings at Town Head (featuring the National Trust's Townhead Barn) the road begins to climb: you soon leave it by a gate signposted on the right, with the majestic Cove already in full view directly ahead. *The popularity of the approach to Malham Cove is evidenced by the strengthened path to cope with the incredible numbers of visitors. Unfortunately, but necessarily, the climb up the side is now on a man-made stairway. A selfish thought maybe, but why couldn't this natural gem be half a dozen miles from the nearest road?*

A path leads to the very foot of the cliffs. *The limestone wall of Malham Cove rises 300 feet from the valley floor: imagine the waterfall that once plunged over here? Issuing from the base is Malham Beck.* To progress further, retrace steps a little to climb the man-made steps round the left side of the Cove. A kissing-gate at the top leads to the extensive limestone pavement covering the Cove-top. *Fascinating to tread, caution is needed on crossing it, for the grikes in between have leg-damaging capabilities.*

Having reached the end of the pavement at the centre of the Cove top a wall is met. Ignore both the stile and the gate however, and follow your side of the wall away from the Cove. After a stile in an intervening wall the crags on either side close in as you proceed along the floor of Watlowes, the Dry Valley. *Comb Hill and Dean Moor Hill form the impressive twin portals at its head. These lofty cliffs - really tiers of small crags - beckon you along Watlowes' deep rugged confines. With this at one end and the Cove top at the other, Watlowes is some little valley!*

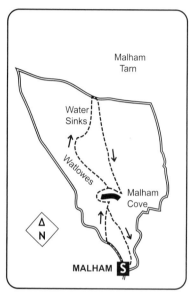

At the valley-head the path escapes by rising to a stile in front, from where it swings sharply right to round a ledge under Dean Moor Hill. *An 80ft waterfall once plunged over the cliffs here.* As the outcrops are left behind a wall provides company across the open moor to lead unfailingly to Water Sinks.

At Water Sinks the outflow from Malham Tarn, for its brief existence known as Malham Water, disappears deep into the ground. It does not return to the surface again for more than two miles, finally appearing at Aire Head Springs (see WALK 4). A common misconception was that it re-appeared at the base of the Cove, but chemical tests long since disproved this theory: just one of the many wonders of this limestone district! Also on arrival at Water Sinks, Malham Tarn House comes into view (but not the tarn itself).

The road across the moor is soon reached at a kissing-gate by following the beck upstream. *From the open road across the moor, the walk could be extended to incorporate the tarn (see WALK 9).* Turn right through Water Sinks Gate on the road, and leave by a path on the right opposite the car park. This (with two variations that soon rejoin) slants gently up across the pasture. *Here you have your only view of the tarn, backed by Fountains Fell.* A wall-stile puts you into the extensive sheep pasture of Prior Rakes, passing some pools. *These are former dewponds, created by the monks to help slake their cattle's thirst.* Head on to the next wall to enter and pass through the well defined trench of Trougate between low limestone outcrops. Past further intervening walls another path is met. Follow this back down to the right to return to the wall at the top of Malham Cove.

Re-cross the limestone pavement and return to the foot of the Cove. Use the path back to Malham as far as the first gate, and then cross the beck by means of a footbridge of stone slabs. Turn right up the slope, and a faint path rises towards the first of three stiles in cross-walls. Continue on to a gap in a collapsing wall, and then follow the wall to the right to reach a stile. *The collapsed walls hereabouts are the remains of Iron Age field boundaries, and must be left alone.* After a few enclosed yards, head away in the same direction with a wall now on the left. On reaching a small shelter, the way becomes enclosed again, and remains so to re-enter Malham in fine style. Debouching onto a back lane, continue straight down past the youth hostel into the village centre.

The head of the Dry Valley

4

AIRE HEAD SPRINGS

START Malham   Grid ref. SD 900626

DISTANCE 3^3_4 miles (6km)

ORDNANCE SURVEY MAPS
1:50,000
Landranger 98 - Wensleydale & Upper Wharfedale
1:25,000
Explorer OL2 - Yorkshire Dales South/West

ACCESS Start from the village centre. National Park car park. Served by Skipton-Malham bus.

> *Absorbing riverbank features lead to a lovely old village*

Leave the information centre for the village, but within yards take a stile on the right, where the road and beck meet. With a wall in between follow the beck downstream, with kissing-gates either side of a slate slab footbridge on Tranlands Beck. As the beck swings away left, continue straight on to arrive at the emerging waters (or not, depending on water levels!) of Aire Head Springs. *This is the point of resurgence of the stream that last saw the light of day at Water Sinks high on the moor (see WALK 3). It is not, therefore, the source of the Aire, but is certainly the first naming of the river. Almost immediately downstream, its waters - which after heavy rain become one mighty spring - join the newly merged Malham and Gordale Becks to flow in unison as the Aire. Look back, also, to see the Cove well presented.*

From the stile just beyond continue alongside the wall. The next stile returns you nearer the river, by now having merged with the beck. An improving path leads above the old millpond. *Now a bird haven, the extensive pond remains in good condition, as does the leat that you follow along to the mill.* The continuing leat leads unfailingly on to Scalegill Mill. *This former manorial mill is now a private dwelling. There has been a mill on this site at least since the 11th century, as it was mentioned in the Domesday Book. It has been used in turn for processing corn, wool, flax and cotton, which in the early 19th century made it Kirkby Malham's major employer. The waterwheel was removed in 1925, turbines being installed for generating electricity.* Pass round the top side of it to a kissing-gate above its entrance gate.

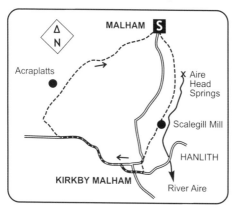

Instead of following the drive away, take the pronounced grass rake sloping up to a stile. *This is the old millworkers' route from the village.* Head half-right across a large field to locate a wall-stile. *Note the attractive grouping of Hanlith over to the left.* Advance on towards the road as it enters Kirkby Malham. Don't join it, but walk parallel with it over the wall. A stile by a gate at the end admits to the road, but to avoid traffic on a narrow bend, go left along the walled lane. This bends round to the Hanlith road, turning right on it to enter the village centre.

Kirkby Malham is, ecclesiastically, the main village of Malhamdale, although most visitors to the valley drive through almost without notice on their way to the tourist Mecca of Malham. This tiny village is however worth exploration, the parish church is of most interest. Dedicated to St Michael the Archangel, this highly attractive building dates from the 15th century and was restored in Victorian times, thanks mainly to Walter Morrison of Malham Tarn House: his memorial can be seen in the church. Also of note are a Norman font and a 16th century German window. Oliver Cromwell is reputed to have signed the register as witnessing a marriage during his stay in the district during the Civil War.

In the churchyard is the base of an ancient preaching cross, and near the lych-gate are the former village stocks. The church is sandwiched between two other buildings of note, the pub at the bridge-end and the immensely attractive vicarage. The Victoria is a pleasant hostelry which does its best to waylay Malham-bound visitors, and features a sundial of 1840 (in Latin) above the door. The old vicarage has a three-storey porch dated 1622, and was restored in 1866. Running alongside is Kirkby Beck, which joins the Aire a good quarter-mile from the village. Further up the lane is the Old Hall.

Kirkby Malham church

From the crossroads by the pub head up the back lane past the church, and round to a T-junction. Turn up the road to the left, the severe gradients ensuring rapid height gain. *Compensation is to be found in the unfolding views, including the Malham scene over to the right: ahead is Pikedaw. This provides an excellent insight into the topography of the area, with Kirkby Fell and Weets Top guarding each side of the valley, and Malham,*

the Cove and the heights of the moor in between. A farm road to New Close is passed before turning right along the Acraplatts farm road. *Bracing views look over the entire upper dale now: the prospect of rugged Pikedaw is particularly impressive*. A little beyond a cattle-grid, before a belt of trees take a stile on the right. Descend to another wall-stile, then pass a ruined barn to a slate slab footbridge over Tranlands Beck (again).

From it cross the field beneath the farm without losing height, to reach a wall-stile at the wooded head of another tiny beck. From it, rise gently to another stile. *This is a superb moment as Malham's setting is revealed in its amphitheatre of hills: Kirkby Fell and Pikedaw offer a dramatic contrast just up to your left.* Follow the wall down to a gate/stile by a barn, and around with the wall to another gate/stile in the corner beyond to enter a large pasture. *While enjoying the great, sweeping vista, note the strip lynchets on the opposite slope between Cove and village, and the haphazard pattern of the drystone walls behind.* Drop down to find a gate in the very bottom. An enclosed way heads down past a barn conversion, joining its drive which runs a pleasant enclosed course all the way down into Malham, emerging next to the car park.

Scalegill Mill

WEETS TOP

START *Malham   Grid ref. SD 900626*

DISTANCE *7^{1}2 miles (11km)*

ORDNANCE SURVEY MAPS
1:50,000
Landranger 98 - Wensleydale & Upper Wharfedale
1:25,000
Explorer OL2 - Yorkshire Dales South/West

ACCESS *Start from the village centre. National Park car park. Served by Skipton-Malham bus.*

A richly varied walk featuring waterfall, moorland, riverbank, an ancient cross, extensive views.... and Gordale Scar

From the car park head into the village, crossing the beck either by a footbridge by the forge, or by the road bridge and then double back to follow the beck downstream. When the short lane ends, a broad path heads across the fields. At a double kissing-gate the path swings left to a barn (the fainter way straight ahead is your return route), crosses to the left of the wall and continues in the same direction. *The outer portals of Gordale Scar as yet reveal nothing of its grandeur: Malham Cove, however, shows itself off back over the village.*

Soon, on entering a delightful section of woodland, the charming waterfall of Janet's Foss is reached. *Legend has it that Janet, local fairy queen, had a cave behind the falls. What is more certain is that this wood provides a rich habitat for a wide variety of flora and fauna: an information board is provided.* Here the path breaks off left to emerge onto the road to Gordale. Turn right along it for a short distance, crossing the beck (by way of the old bridge if you wish) and arriving at a gate on the left just before Gordale House. *The Augustinian canons of Bolton Priory once owned Gordale, and traces of foundations close to the path mark the site of a building where they held a manorial court.* A well trodden path crosses the pasture to the unmistakable cliffs of Gordale Scar, which converge as you enter the dark confines. *Gordale Scar is probably the most awe-inspiring single feature of the Yorkshire Dales: for more on it see WALK 8.*

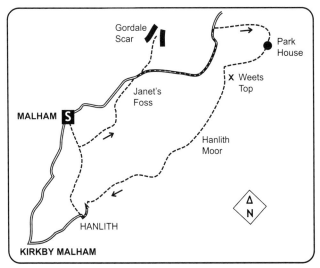

Back out on the road, continue past Gordale House to commence the climb up cul-de-sac Hawthorns Lane. The country to either side displays the classic contrast caused by the Craven Fault, with distinctive limestone country on the left and sombre gritstone terrain to the right. *After the gradients have eased you have the option of a shorter variant saving a good mile. This turns off right along a walled track which makes the short climb to Weets Cross.*

For the full walk remain on the road a little further, now completely level to find an initially enclosed farm drive to the right. *Fountains Fell appears over to the left above the limestone uplands, with Great Whernside similarly placed ahead.* Follow this all the way to Park House. *En route you can enjoy an appraisal of the limestone heights surrounding Bordley, with Greenhow Hill, Simon's Seat and Barden Moor ahead.* At the gaunt farmstead pass through the gate into its confines and round to the yard proper. The house bears a 1686 datestone. From a gate after the house rise through another into a field, then ascend its side to a wall-stile at the top into scattered upland trees. A nice path rises and runs to a like stile at the end. The path then traces a wall to a stile at the end, before a pathless crossing to a wall-stile onto the Weets lane. *En route there is a splendid appearance of Ingleborough ahead.*

Absorbing the short-cut option, turn left for the very brief climb to Weets Cross. *The restored cross marks the meeting point of numerous old township boundaries.* Through the gate adjacent to it will be found, just up to the left, the Ordnance Survey column crowning Weets Top. *At 1358ft/414m Weets Top is one of the finest viewpoints in the area, with most features in the southern Dales in sight: mighty Ingleborough is the finest landmark, some others are mentioned in the previous and ensuing paragraphs.*

Weets Cross

Returning to the gate a good path heads away, at once forking. Keep right to begin a gentle descent of the moor. Soon approaching a guidepost a grassy branch bears right to slant down to a gate in the nearby wall. From it a partly moist, occasionally vague path begins a stride across Hanlith Moor, close by the wall on the left before swinging gently right. *Far ahead are the South Pennines, Pendle Hill, the Ribble Valley, Grindleton Fell and the Bowland moors, while closer to hand are fine Malhamdale limestone features in front of*

Fountains Fell, with Malham village appearing. Ultimately the route drops to a corner gate off the moor, through which the rough track of Windy Pike Lane descends unfailingly into Hanlith. *During this Malham village and Cove are regular features, with a wide sweep of most of Malhamdale: Kirkby Fell and Pikedaw present the dramatic change from gritstone to limestone. There is also a fine prospect of Kirkby Malham across the river, its church prominent.*

Don't drop all the way to the river, but at the second sharp bend in Hanlith take a small gate on the right above a farm. Cross a small enclosure to a gate, on above the farm to contour across the field. *Remarkably the mighty Pennine Way, within a mile of busy Malham, is barely discernable underfoot. Malham Cove is directly ahead now, with the entrance to Gordale to the right. Across the river note the distinctive strip lynchets (ancient cultivation terraces) beneath the dale's school.*

At the end of the field you are channeled into a gate to continue along a wood-top to a kissing-gate overlooking a grand Malham scene fronted by the river. In the next field contour to and across a hollow to rise to another kissing-gate before descending to the lovely confluence of Malham Beck and Gordale Beck. Use a footbridge on the latter, and from a kissing-gate cross to rejoin the outward leg, and retrace those first steps back into the village.

Janet's Foss

6

FOUNTAINS FELL

START *Malham Tarn*   *Grid ref. SD 883671*

DISTANCE *8$\frac{1}{2}$ miles (13$\frac{1}{2}$km)*

ORDNANCE SURVEY MAPS
1:50,000
Landranger 98 - Wensleydale & Upper Wharfedale
1:25,000
Explorer OL2 - Yorkshire Dales South/West

ACCESS *Start from a parking area in an old quarry on the Arncliffe road just south of Water Houses, west of Malham Tarn. Nearby seasonal Settle-Malham weekend minibus •OPEN ACCESS: see page 6.*

One of Craven's bulky moorland mountains gives excellent views of the Three Peaks from its sometimes rough terrain

Turn right along the road very briefly, then double sharply back left along a walled track. This runs on past the nature reserve of Tarn Moss to meet an access road at the estate cottages of Water Houses. Turn right, briefly, then take a gate on the left from where a footpath heads off. *Here you join the Pennine Way almost to the summit of Fountains Fell.* Beyond a gate/stile the path runs a clear wallside course. *En route, a clever little barn is passed, with three entrances each accessing different fields; Darnbrook Fell appears ahead, soon joined by Fountains Fell.* Always keep the wall to the left, twice cutting corners before arriving at a ladder-stile, then converging with the wall to stride grandly on. *Fountains Fell now spreads its broad shoulders, with your immediate objective of Tennant Gill Farm straight ahead.* Dropping to a right-angle bend of the wall go with it down to a gate/stile. Now bear right on a thin path across the field to rejoin the unfenced road.

Cross straight over and along the drive to Tennant Gill. *Above are limestone tors that will shortly give way to the upper gritstone reaches of Fountains Fell. Already you enjoy a sweeping view over Darnbrook and Cowside to Great Whernside.* Without entering the yard turn left up the track, and level with the upper buildings a gentle grass track climbs to a gate/stile onto the open fell. A good path bears left, rapidly swinging right to ascend alongside the vestiges of a wall. This smashing green way climbs for some time before swinging right to run a more level course to a gate in a descending wall. *If you haven't looked back yet, do now to espy Malham Tarn backed by the miniature peaks of Flasby Fell.*

The restored path continues as an intermittently green and then firmer way. *As more height is gained the views extend, with under-ling Darnbrook Fell just in front and Great Whernside the dominant force amid a barrage of higher ground towards Wharfedale.* After a steeper section the going eases and the track runs along to its summit, where a pair of stone men stand alongside old mining spoil just to the right. At this point the watershed wall appears, as does Penyghent. *The 'Lion of Ribblesdale' is ably supported by its loftier brethren Ingleborough and Whernside.*

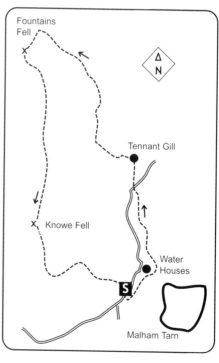

At this point leave the Pennine Way and take a lesser but still clear path left past a prominent fenced shaft, bound for the summit of Fountains Fell just a few level minutes away. *Be sure to resist peering down into the mineshafts that abound, they are extremely deep. Fountains Fell's upper reaches are dotted with various mining remains, for both coal and lead were won here and spoilheaps abound. The colliery was at its peak in the early 19th century, and your route of ascent has been along the old colliers' way.* Just yards further is a stone hut known as the 'Igloo'. *This curious feature was erected by miners as a coke oven.*

Beyond the Igloo bear right at a fork, and the grooved track runs quickly to the summit mound, where a thin path climbs left to the cairn. At 2172ft/662m the summit is surmounted by a solid pile of stones, though less imposing than it once was. *In the magnificent panorama, Whernside and Wild Boar Fell are visible from the path but hidden from the summit view. Major features, working clockwise, are: Ingleborough, Penyghent, Whernside, Howgill Fells, Baugh Fell, Plover Hill, Wild Boar Fell, Cross Fell, Great Dun Fell, High Seat, Dodd Fell, Little Fell, Mickle Fell, Great Shunner Fell, Wether Fell, Lovely Seat, Rogan's Seat, Yockenthwaite Moor, Birks Fell, Buckden Pike, Little Whernside, Great Whernside, Meugher, Grassington Moor, Parson's Pulpit, Simon's Seat, Barden Moor, Skipton Moor, Rombalds Moor, Grizedales, Rye Loaf Hill, Pendle Hill, Grindleton Fell, White Hill and eastern Bowland, and Ward's Stone, highest point in Bowland.*

Leave on a thin path south-east indicated by the first of several posts, your goal being the gentle rise of the South top across a modest hollow. Fountains Fell Tarn quickly appears to your left, a substantial sheet of water given its lofty location. The path soon converges with the wall from the right to trace it up onto the brow of the South Top, and remains with the wall as you gently decline. *Malham Tarn is in view straight ahead, and will remain so for much of the return.* Dropping to a sturdy wall junction, a stile crosses to an area of scattered boulders. Turn right with the wall to the corner, negotiate a fence then descend gently again with the crumbling wall. Progress is marginally better on the other side, until down in a dip the fence returns. The going is less enamouring as vague path, old wall and fence shuffle together along the fell, keeping east of the watershed. Ahead is a minor knoll, atop which things improve. Continue as before, now on the watershed with better conditions underfoot, further eased as limestone turf leads the intermittent path to the beckoning OS column on Knowe Fell.

At 1945ft/593m this marks a super viewpoint for the well proportioned Three Peaks. On leaving cross to the wall corner just behind. Cross the fence and the left-hand wall, then turn right with the now sturdy wall to resume a watershed descent of the fell on a modest path. *Rye Loaf Hill presents a distinctive dome ahead.* Part way down, after a lone shakehole, Malham Tarn is glimpsed and an optional short-cut presents itself - *simply slant across to join the already visible return bridleway slanting up to a limestone scar.* Otherwise follow the wall down to a gate/stile in it. Double back sharply left on a grassy path, slanting gently up above a tiny sidestream towards a prominent limestone scar on the skyline. On the brow the path briefly fades, passing left of the quarried scar onto this limestone knoll, another good viewpoint for Malham Tarn.

The path returns to drop past scattered outcrops towards a wall corner. Head away with the wall on your right. At a minor dip take a slate stile built into the wall just as it becomes sturdier and follow a thin trod directly away, with a tussocky area on your right. Crossing a quad track forge on, the trod fading as it points to limestone rocks just ahead. Using the left edge of the tarn as guide bear gently left, declining through scattered rocks to espy a cairn on a grassy knoll ahead. This makes a splendid final viewpoint over the tarn and moss. Drop steeply to pick up a cross-path below and turn left, contouring round the slope and angling down above the old quarry to a gate at the foot of a wall. This deposits you onto the road just a couple of minutes beyond the quarry.

Ordnance Survey column on Knowe Fell, looking to Penyghent

STOCKDALE

START *Water Sinks Gate*   *Grid ref. SD 893657*

DISTANCE *9¹2 miles (15km)*

ORDNANCE SURVEY MAPS
1:50,000
Landranger 98 - Wensleydale & Upper Wharfedale
1:25,000
Explorer OL2 - Yorkshire Dales South/West

ACCESS *Start from a roadside car park on the road crossing the Malham Tarn outflow. Seasonal Settle-Malham weekend minibus.*

A high level march into the territory of Ribblesdale without the effort of descending into it: largely crowd-free

Leave the car park by taking Water Sinks Gate over Malham Water emerging from the unseen tarn, and head west along the road for the best part of a mile, the first half having a useful verge. *On the left is a smelt mill chimney restored by Earby Mines Research Group in the 1970s. Fountains Fell sprawls across to the right.* At the junction with the Malham-Langcliffe road take a stile/gate on the left, just across. Bear half-right to a stile/gate out of the fenced enclosure, then bear left on a path that fords a muddy stream before rising pleasantly to a stile/gate at a wall junction. A thin way continues alongside the crumbling wall on your right, and just before a corner it bears left through another collapsed wall and over a limestone brow to find a stile/gate in the sturdy wall ahead. A thin path heads away through the partly moist, extensive pasture of Gorbeck.

Things improve as Ingleborough, Queen of Yorkshire's mountains appears ahead. Whernside's whaleback appears to its right, with a clear day revealing Black Combe some 50 miles distant on the horizon. And then, like a ghost ship silently floating into harbour, mighty Penyghent moves in. From the moment of its first appearance until its disappearance, Penyghent rules the roost. This Pennine moorland scene is now far removed from Malham's orderliness, a stark contrast indeed. Towards the far end Gorbeck Road is joined and a pleasant, clear track ensues. In recent years this has been substantially upgraded to carry a Pennine Bridleway Loop, sections previously having been desecrated by 4x4 use. This same track remains underfoot for a considerable time, and leaving the harsher terrain behind a grassy section is enjoyed before a firmer track returns, now with a wall permanently on the right.

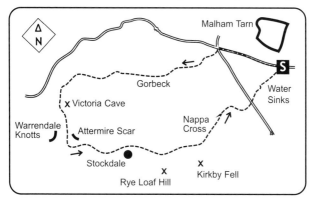

As progress is made the mountain panorama includes Ingleborough, Great Coum, Whernside, the dome of Yarlside popping up from the Howgill Fells, Baugh Fell, Penyghent, Plover Hill and Fountains Fell. On a clear day the distant prospect of Caw and the Coniston Fells is revealed to the left of Ingleborough.

The old road winds down. *Ahead are the Bowland moors, then round the corner the Settle hills just ahead: Pendle Hill appears through a gap.* Beyond a stile on the right, the track runs on to a gate. Don't descend any further but take a kissing-gate on the left which sends a level path along to approach Victoria Cave, hidden up to the left. *Before approaching it consider the warnings of the perils of rockfalls. The cave is very definitely not hidden when you gain it, for it boasts an enormous entrance. Though the cave's entrance has been blasted to this size in modern times, its history goes back through countless periods. Evidence of a richly varied occupancy has been yielded, including bones of rhinoceros, hippopotamus, bear and mammoth, and also Stone Age man.*

Victoria Cave

Beyond a kissing-gate at the end the main path soon runs on through open pasture with the contorted tors of Warrendale Knotts on the right. Further, it drops steeply to a gateway beneath the impressive Attermire Scar. *Two minutes through the gateway will earn a better appraisal of Warrendale Knotts. Attermire Cave is to be found within the scar, a dark slit located high up the limestone cliff.* Here the main path heads off right through the gateway, bound for Settle. Your equally inviting grassy path swings left to contour round beneath Attermire Scar. The way rises through several pastures - gates all the way - to emerge onto surfaced Stockdale Lane: go left. *Views across this secluded side valley are dominated by Rye Loaf Hill's rounded dome.*

This is classic Craven Fault country - millstone grit to the right, with you still very much amid limestone. Don't take the road to Stockdale Farm, but use a gate on the left as a track continues above the wall. *Note the farm's isolation: though no distance from Settle, it is the only settlement in its own valley.* The track runs on and on, gently up to reach its zenith. From the highest gate a level section ensues to approach a large cairn. *Although this is a pass, it is virtually as high as the hills through which it runs. Revealed ahead is a wonderful prospect of Malham Tarn and Moor, and more distantly Buckden Pike and Great Whernside.*

Nappa Gate is immediately behind the cairn. Here the old way commences its descent, but don't pass through: instead, turn left with the wall on a path running to Nappa Cross at the corner just ahead. *This is one of several wayside crosses in the area, a guidepost for travellers since monastic times. Set into the wall, the restored shaft stands in its original base.*

Beyond the cross a broad grassy way slopes down to a gate, maintaining the slant through further pastures to meet the grassy Gorbeck Road at a corner. Turn right down this to descend to the road out of the village at Langscar Gate. Cross the cattle-grid and turn off the open road by a grassy path on the right. This rises through a gap and on through a gateway in a wall, then on again over Dean Moor to see the start point just ahead. Also seen just below, to the right, is Water Sinks (see WALK 3). The path slants down to run on to a kissing-gate onto the road at Water Sinks Gate.

Rye Loaf Hill from Stockdale

GORDALE SCAR

START *Water Sinks Gate*   *Grid ref. SD 893657*

DISTANCE *6 miles (9½km)*

ORDNANCE SURVEY MAPS
1:50,000
Landranger 98 - Wensleydale & Upper Wharfedale
1:25,000
Explorer OL2 - Yorkshire Dales South/West

ACCESS *Start from a roadside car park on the road crossing the Malham Tarn outflow. Seasonal Settle-Malham weekend minibus.*

An awesome ravine is centrepiece of a splendid limestone walk

> *Note that at Gordale Scar one needs to partake of a short climb on rock - this is a fairly simple task with ample handholds, but may be outside the scope of less-agile walkers. It is beyond all non-amphibious walkers after a good deal of rain. The alternatives are mentioned during the text.*

Leave the car park by crossing the road and head south on a path slanting gently left (with two variations that soon rejoin) to a stile in the wall ahead, meeting another path at this point. Across, the path enters Prior Rakes, an extensive sheep pasture recalling the wealthy landowning interests of Fountains Abbey. The path runs quickly on to reach another path junction alongside some pools. *These are dewponds, created in monastic times to help slake the thirsts of cattle in these largely dry limestone uplands.*

Advance alongside the pools, but fork left before they end, on a thinner but clear path rising gently away, with a parallel wall over to the left. Within 75 yards take a right fork to rise very gently alongside a low line of modest rocks, easily followed as it keeps them strictly to one side. The increasingly expansive pavements of Broad Scars feature to the right, while you can look back to the tarn backed by the sombre moor-mountain of Fountains Fell. *The unfolding panorama ahead meanwhile features Barden Moor, Flasby Fell, the South Pennines and island-like Pendle Hill beyond an array of close-at-hand limestone features.*

As the one and only outcrop on your left is reached, the thin path veers left past it and drops down through a band of low outcrops to merge with a broader green path. Bear right on this across Malham Lings, a lovely stride to a stile onto the road just above the start of its steep drop towards Malham village. Turn right and commence the descent. *An early stile on the left gives a short-cut option of dropping straight down alongside some telegraph poles to the through path below.*

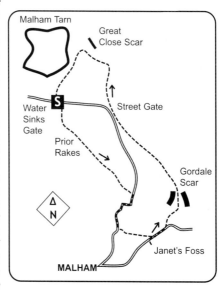

Further down the road a cross-path is met. A firm path heads away from a kissing-gate on the left, curving round (with a view of Malham village) until turning into a field on the right. *Ahead the Craven Fault is perfectly displayed as Hawthorns Lane marks the boundary between sombre gritstone and gleaming limestone, accentuated by the series of parallel walls.* Drop to a kissing-gate below and then down the wallside to a corner, slanting left to a kissing-gate by the old bridge and refreshment van onto the road to Gordale.

First though, make the five-minute detour to see Janet's Foss, turning briefly right to use a path on the left to the beautiful waterfall in its wooded setting. *Legend has it that Janet, local fairy queen, had a cave behind the falls. More certain is that this wood is a rich habitat for a wide variety of flora and fauna.* Back on the road go right, crossing the beck to arrive at a gate on the left just before Gordale House. *The Augustinian canons of Bolton Priory once owned Gordale, and traces of foundations near the path mark the site of a building where they held a manorial court.* A well trodden path crosses the pasture to the unmistakable cliffs of Gordale Scar, which converge as you enter the dark confines.

Gordale Scar is the most awe-inspiring single feature of the Yorkshire Dales. Unlike the Cove at Malham, which bares all on first sighting, the Scar has a far more intriguing nature, waiting for the visitor to turn the final corner before impressing him to the full. Once in its depths the grandeur of the overhanging cliffs up above can initially be too daunting to fully appreciate the waterfalls: the upper fall spills in spectacular fashion through a circular hole in the rocks. The water is that of Gordale Beck, being funneled from the lonely moors to the green valley. Like the cove, this is a valley cut back from the Craven Fault, formed by erosive action of ice and glacial meltwater, rather than being a collapsed cave. Turn a corner and it's there, is there no escape?

The way out is by negotiating the rock to the left of the lower falls. It is a straightforward short scramble with plentiful handholds, but nevertheless care is necessary - please don't fall on anyone. *If it proves impassable, hang your head low and seek an alternative: either latch onto WALK 1 as far as the Cove-top and then trace the Dry Valley (WALK 3) back to the start, or return to Gordale House and ascend Hawthorns Lane to Lee Gate and pick up WALK 10.* On gaining the top of the climb, pause to survey the tremendous scene in this magnificent amphitheatre, including a better prospect of the upper fall dropping through its window.

Having clambered up, the stony path clings to the left side of the gorge, passing the upper falls and breaking out onto green pastures. Running straight ahead is the upper Gordale Valley. Beyond a stile the path runs a delightful and contrastingly easy course across the limestone moor, parallel with the upper valley for some time before a long line of low outcrops deflects it left, and a long trek ensues before arriving at a stile onto the moor road to Malham Tarn. You need not use it, instead remain on the clear path continuing along the wallside to arrive at a stile onto the historic crossroads of Street Gate. *Here the classic green road of Mastiles Lane heads off to the right, explored in WALK 10.*

Pass neither through the gate nor left to the moor road, instead bear right along the wallside Middle House farm road. This runs to a cattle-grid alongside tiny Great Close Plantation. Advance only a little further past the end of the trees and then double back sharply left on a more inviting grassy track. This quickly reaches a minor brow to reveal Malham Tarn ahead. Advance along this super track beneath the mighty limestone cliffs of Great Close Scar to ultimately join the driveway at the tarn edge. Double back left on this to a gate back onto the grassy moor, after which quickly bear right on a broad grassy path past a wood corner. Although this leads directly back to the car park, better to take the right branch from the wood corner to cross to the outflow of the tarn. The path then runs the few minutes downstream with Malham Water to return to the start.

Gordale Scar

DARNBROOK

START *Water Sinks Gate*   Grid ref. SD 893657

DISTANCE *8^{1}2 miles (13^{1}2km)*

ORDNANCE SURVEY MAPS
1:50,000
Landranger 98 - Wensleydale & Upper Wharfedale
1:25,000
Explorer OL2 - Yorkshire Dales South/West

ACCESS *Start from a roadside car park on the road crossing the Malham Tarn outflow. Seasonal Settle-Malham weekend minibus.*

> *Easy walking and big views on the limestone heights above and beyond Malham Tarn*

From the back of the car park a path sets off across the moor. Forking, the left branch runs on to quickly reach Tarn Foot, where Malham Water emerges from Malham Tarn. *Splendid views look over this upland lake to Malham Tarn House in trees beneath Highfolds Scar, with Fountains Fell further left. At 1230ft/375m above sea level, Malham Tarn is an extensive sheet of water: its existence in this limestone preserve is due to the layer of Silurian slate on which it stands. With adjacent wetlands the tarn is home to a rich birdlife. The surrounding calcarious grassland, woodland and limestone pavement further contribute to its status as a National Nature Reserve. It is jointly managed by its owners the National Trust, and the Field Studies Council, who operate at Tarn House. The monks of Fountains Abbey held fishing rights, while Charles Kingsley drew inspiration to create 'The Water Babies'.*

Turn right on a path above the shore to the top end of a walled plantation, and on to merge with the drive at a gate. Follow the drive along the shore of the tarn, passing the cliffs of Great

Close Scar. Do not enter the woods at the cattle-grid, but climb right. *This slope gives excellent views back over the tarn.* A green path materialises to rise to the saddle between Highfolds and Great Close Hill. *This is the Monk's Road, which leaves no doubt as to its original patrons: walkers now stride where packhorses toiled.*

Beyond the gap, the path runs along towards Middle House Farm, but beyond an intervening fence-stile slant left up to a stile by a gate on a brow above the farm. From here a track heads across the limestone pasture, but at an early fork remain on the more inviting way which swings right to join a wall. A cluster of barns at Old Middle House is passed. *Embowered in trees, this was restored in 1990 by the National Trust. Sheep farming here dates from Norse times, before passing into the hands of Fountains Abbey.* The path crosses a collapsed wall to a guidepost: here you leave the Arncliffe path and take the

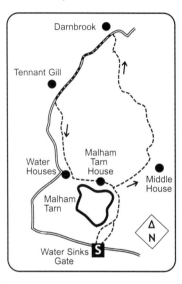

left fork. It contours round the slopes of these wonderful limestone uplands, with a wall coming in on the right: the path is a little faint here. *Ahead you are treated to grand views over to Darnbrook Fell, with Fountains Fell entering the scene on the left.*

A stile crosses the wall, from where the path heads off through more outcrops. *Strongly evident on the brow are the pronounced wall patterns of an ancient British settlement.* From here the distinct grassy path commences a long, gentle descent of a vast sweeping slope, with the hidden farm at Darnbrook soon appearing ahead, nestling in trees. Aiming for the farm, descend to a gateway in the wall below. *A good limestone pavement sits just to your right, a good foreground to views down Cowside Beck to the floor of Littondale backed by Old Cote Moor and, behind, Buckden Pike.*

Bear down to the right of the dry side-valley, faintly now, and from the grassy bank that is the scant remnants of a wall a green way slants down to a stone slab bridge on Cowside Beck. From the stile by the beck head for the barn in front, using a gap behind it to advance across the fields by a further stile and out by a small gate onto the road at Darnbrook. *White-walled Darnbrook House is an isolated and historic farmstead, dating back over 600 years when it had connections with Fountains Abbey. The present building has a 17th century datestone and mullioned windows.*

Turn left along this narrow road for 1¼ miles, some of which can be trodden on open verges. At a sharp left turn by the drive to Tennant Gill Farm on the right, leave the road along a thin but clear path across open pasture on the left to drop to a gate/stile in a wall in the dip. A track climbs beyond it to a wall corner, where turn right to accompany the wall across undulating pastures. Initially faint, the path picks up to remain with or close by the adjacent wall. *En route a clever little barn is passed, with three entrances each accessing different fields.* The last stile leads through a shallow limestone trough, emerging by way of a canopy of trees onto the drive at Water Houses.

Turn left along this track through the wooded grounds of Malham Tarn House. A bird hide and a tarn viewpoint are passed as the drive squeezes between rock walls to reach the rear of the house. *Malham Tarn House was built as a shooting lodge for Lord Ribblesdale, and was much improved by the Morrison family in the 1850s. It is now a long-established field studies centre.* Continue out to the tarn shore that you left so long ago. Retrace your steps to the gate at the entrance, and then bear right on a green path, past the wood corner to cross the moor to the start.

Clapper bridge,
Cowside Beck

MASTILES LANE

START Street Gate   Grid ref. SD 904656

DISTANCE 7 miles (11km)

ORDNANCE SURVEY MAPS
1:50,000
Landranger 98 - Wensleydale & Upper Wharfedale
1:25,000
Explorer OL2 - Yorkshire Dales South/West

ACCESS Street Gate is where Mastiles Lane branches off the Malham-Malham Tarn road (the road east of the Cove). Verge parking at the junction. Seasonal Settle-Malham weekend minibus.

A fine upland ramble with a good dose of history and big views

Head east away from the junction along the tarmac start of Mastiles Lane to the historic crossroads of Street Gate. *Mastiles Lane is probably the best known of the district's old roads. The classic green lane was used by the monks of Fountains Abbey to cross from Kilnsey to their valuable sheep-rearing pastures in the Malham area, indeed, connecting ultimately to their lands in Borrowdale, in distant Cumberland. Packmen and drovers would also have take advantage of it. The lane is at its most inspiring when fully enclosed by walls, though the monks would not have known it that way. Several large boulders incorporated into the lane's north wall are boundary stones separating Malham and Bordley.* Pass through the gate and follow the lane in its various guises for rather less than three miles.

The walking is easy and pleasant as the track clings to the right-hand wall. A big dip takes in the upper reaches of Gordale Beck, with an old clapper-bridge in attendance. At a gate the way becomes confined, and enjoys another good spell before becoming part open again at the end. Simply forge on its delightful course amid archetypal, rolling limestone uplands. Beyond another gate it rises gently, hugging the left-hand wall. *The brow has views to Barden Moor, Flasby Fell and the South Pennines.*

At Mastiles Gate it becomes enclosed again: don't pass through but finally abandon the lane by turning right on a faint wallside track through a hollow, a grand stride to a junction with the end of a surfaced road: cross straight over, through a gate, and up the access road to Bordley. *On the brow the hamlet suddenly appears at your feet, nestling in its folds of the hills: down-valley, Winterburn Reservoir is backed by Flasby Fell.* The road becomes surfaced again to drop into the hamlet. *Bordley is a lonely outpost where sheep farming continues much as in its days as a monastic township. Stood at a breezy near-1100 feet above sea level, its solid stone buildings spread around a large green, sheltered from the weather's worst extremes by virtue of its position in a hollow.*

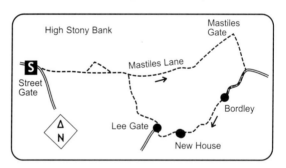

Leave by a gate in the far left corner, alongside a barn bearing a lintel dated 1664. Cross the small field to a gate ahead, then keep faith with a faint track with the left-hand wall. *Views ahead look to Barden Moor, Flasby Fell and close to hand Weets Top.* This ultimately swings round in a further field until a crumbling corner is reached. Bear left to a wall-stile just short of the corner, then turn right through a gate in the corner. Resume with the left-hand wall until it drops away above the beginnings of Heber Beck. A little grooved path maintains the contour to cross the beginnings of the stream and up to a corner stile above. Rise right with the wall to a small gate near the corner, then slant up to a small gate just past the attractive farmhouse at New House Farm.

Go left along its access road whch rises to a brow then drops down to Lee Gate Farm. *The brow gives views back to Barden Moor, with Weets Top to the left and Kirkby Fell ahead.* Continue out to a junction of lanes just beyond, where the surfaced access road of Smearbottoms Lane swings left. Instead, take a gate in front and bear right along the extensive field, initially on a wall-side track. When this turns into a field simply keep faith with the wall to ultimately arrive back on Mastiles Lane.

Turn left through the gate and retrace steps to the start, ideally incorporating the following minor detour. Leave the track after only five minutes, alongside the stone platform of a covered reservoir. The initially faint grassy path angles only gradually away from the wall, improving and broadening to drop gently down towards to a reedy pool. Right alongside is the distinctive grassy bank of a Roman camp, which you can trace back left to the lane. Rejoining, very quickly and not more than 15 yards distant to your right is an ancient cross base.

Mastiles Lane

CALTON MOOR

START *Calton*   *Grid ref. SD 908591*

DISTANCE *8¾ miles (14km)*

ORDNANCE SURVEY MAPS
1:50,000
Landranger 98 - Wensleydale & Upper Wharfedale
Landranger 103 - Blackburn & Burnley
1:25,000
Explorer OL2 - Yorkshire Dales South/West

ACCESS *Start from the cul-de-sac street just off the Airton-Hetton road. Roadside parking taking care not to block any access. Calton is only ten minutes walk from Airton, served by Skipton-Malham bus.*

An ideal Bank Holiday walk for Malhamdale, for while you won't entirely avoid the crowds, you'll miss most of them

Calton is a sleepy hamlet, but with some history: the original Calton Hall was the home of John Lambert, one of Cromwell's generals during the Civil War. At the end of the short-lived street, turn right along a rough lane past Nelsons Farm. *This runs on between hedgerows with nice views over the lower dale to Pendle Hill.* At a squat, modern barn bear left, the way rising to quickly emerge into a field.

Keep straight on by the short wall ahead, and reaching a fence corner bear left to a small gate in the fence ahead. *Views ahead open out to bring in more of the South Pennines alongside Pendle.* Beyond this make for the barn of Farlands Laithe. From a gate just before it, bear gently right to a small gate in the fence ahead. Your next objective is the farm of Cowper Cote ahead. *By now you have a wondrous prospect of Barden Moor and Flasby Fell ahead.* After dropping to a stile alongside an intervening trickle, head up the field to a gate in a section of wall above the farm.

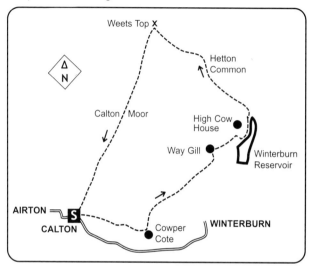

Advance just a few steps then turn up the large domed field on a faint tractor way, bearing right near the end to find a gate just short of the corner. An improving green way continues, bearing right to stay near a fence on an embankment. Beyond another gate the thinner continuation remains near the fence, descending at the end to a gateway just above the bottom corner, above a small wood. Turn up to the prominent barn of Windros Laithe, going round it to find a stile below the small plantation. Up the brow beyond take a gate/stile on the right to join a firm track. This goes left to pass through the wall at the end, then through a second successive gate runs on to the isolated house at Smither Gill Laithe. Absorbing its drive climb away to swing right to a junction.

Go left towards Way Gill Farm, but without entering its yard cross the field to a gate to the right of the house. Bear gently left down the field, with Winterburn Reservoir now laid out ahead. At the bottom a stile admits onto another farm road. This goes left to High Cow House, but you leave it before the farm, at a wall-stile on the right. Head down the fieldside to approach the reservoir. At the bottom turn left for a delightful ramble alongside the shore, and on through several fields above the reservoir's upper reach to arrive at a stone arched bridge over Bordley Beck before it enters the reservoir. *Beneath a fence shortly before it, a stone inscribed LLC indicates the reservoir was constructed to supply the Leeds-Liverpool Canal at Gargrave.*

Winterburn Reservoir is a substantial finger-like sheet of water which at times could be mistaken for being natural. Even the dam with its grass cover seems to blend in: the old keeper's house has been restored. A variety of birdlife takes advantage of this peaceful setting. The head of the reservoir points to extensive moor-like terrain, and a fine spot for a five-minute break.

Resume without crossing the bridge by taking a gate on the left, from where a path rises away with the wall through rough pasture. Here begins the lengthy but exceedingly well-graded climb to Weets Top. Never far from the wall, the splendid path rises to a gate at the top. Having just acquired a more solid surface it then curves right through a reedy pasture to another gate. Through this it returns to grassy status, rising then curving right around the field top to regain its modern surface. Through a gate in the far corner moorland proper is entered, and the firm track remains underfoot all the way to the top. *Looking back the reservoir forms a pleasing sight, backed by the little peaks of Flasby Fell.*

A wall comes up from the left to rise together to a brow under Hetton Common Head: this short spell enjoys a delectable grassy surface to reach a gate. *Ahead now is the long awaited view into Malhamdale, and it's a cracker: the show-stealer though is the appearance of mighty Ingleborough in the gap between Grizedales and Fountains Fell. Great Whernside also eases its broad shoulders into place across to the right.* Five minutes ahead is the 'parent' top Weets Top, marked by an OS column, and a hard path duly runs to the gate beneath it. Just through the gate is Weets Cross. *The restored cross marks the meeting point of a number of township boundaries (see page 22). At 1358ft/414m Weets Top is one of the finest viewpoints in the area, with most features in the southern Dales in sight: mighty Ingleborough is the finest landmark, some others are mentioned in the previous and ensuing paragraphs.*

Leave the gate by doubling sharply back to the left, the path immediately forking. Ignore your arrival route and now bear right to commence a prolonged descent of Calton Moor on a restored surface with a wall close by on the right. Ignore a branch right at an early guidepost and simply retain this firm path which proves to be a splendid leg-stretcher, forever losing height at the most gentle of rates. *Views to the left feature Barden Moor, and to the right the Malhamdale hills around Kirkby Fell.*

The path eventually reaches a gate/stile in a cross-wall. Beyond that the limestone wall on the right soon parts company, but the now grassy and occasionally faint way keeps straight on over a large sheep pasture, curving right to descend above a wooded gill on the left. *Airton's houses appear just ahead, as shortly do some of Calton's.* Descending to a corner by some sheep pens the track becomes enclosed and continues as a leafy rough lane. Fording the sometimes dry beck it quickly climbs back to the road end where the walk began.

Winterburn Reservoir

KIRKBY MALHAM

START *Airton*   *Grid ref. SD 902591*

DISTANCE *4³4 miles (7¹2km)*

ORDNANCE SURVEY MAPS
1:50,000
Landranger 98 - Wensleydale & Upper Wharfedale
Landranger 103 - Blackburn & Burnley
1:25,000
Explorer OL2 - Yorkshire Dales South/West

ACCESS *Start from the village centre. Roadside parking, don't impinge upon the green. Served by Skipton-Malham bus.*

A gentle ramble over rolling hills, with a superb riverbank walk

For a note on Airton see page 50. Leave the green by the telephone box at the south-west corner, crossing the main road and up the road opposite, signed to Hellifield. *This attractive corner is Town End - note the old water pump by the roadside just past Manor Farm.* Shortly after the last buildings take a gate on the right, with another one just behind it. *Already, you have a first view of Malham Cove ahead.* Head away along the field-edge, transferring to the other side of a fence when the wall turns away. A sunken way continues to a barn conversion (1862 datestone on window lintel), passing to its left to emerge onto Scosthrop Lane.

Turn left up this pleasant lane until a more level section is encountered. Take a gate on the left at some sheep pens and head across the field, angling steadily away from the wall. Just short of the corner at the far end is a gate close by a small stone hut, Dowber Laithe. Head away on a modest trod, passing beneath a small old quarry enveloped in larches to arrive at a stile in the facing wall close by the left corner. *From here to Kirkby Malham your walk follows an old way known as the Kirk Gait. As its name suggests, it is the route taken by the good folk of Otterburn (see WALK 14) to Kirkby Malham church. A glimpse at the OS map will confirm the practical, direct way they chose.* Across the stile, pass through another to your right and follow the right-hand wall away. When it parts company continue over the brow of the field. *This modest brow is a super vantage point, with the Barden Moor skyline over to the right featuring prominently, with Rye Loaf Hill and Kirkby Fell ahead, Pendle Hill*

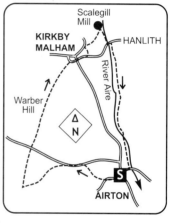

far behind and the Otterburn Moor landscape over to the left. Pick out a ladder-stile in the wall ahead, bearing left towards it to emerge back onto Scosthrop Lane.

Cross to a stile opposite and ascend the wallside. *Enjoy a view back to Pendle Hill and the Craven lowlands, and east to the Barden Moor edges and Flasby Fell. Over the wall, note the impressive stone arch at the site of an old quarry.* Pass left of a small wood to a stile on the brow of Warber Hill, and down by the wall leading away. *This descent gives a good view of the setting of Malhamdale, with all the hills around the valley head to be seen. Features include Rye Loaf Hill, Kirkby Fell, Pikedaw, Fountains Fell, Malham Cove, Malham Moor, the portals of Gordale Scar, Weets Top, Hanlith Moor, and right in front of you, the old Kirk Gait.*

Go down to a wall-stile at the bottom, beyond which a tiny stone bridge crosses a tiny beck. From it leave the wall and bear across the field along an initially shallow but fading groove. Cross to the far end aiming for a clump of trees, where a stile puts you on a farm track. Kirkby Malham is revealed quite dramatically at your feet, with the church tower pre-eminent. Cross straight over and descend outside a wood. From a stile at the bottom slant right to one in the wall opposite, continuing the direction to reach a bridle-gate to enter trees below. Steps descend to a footbridge on Kirkby Beck, then up onto a lane by the church. *For notes on Kirkby Malham, please refer to WALK 4.*

The River Aire above Airton

Turn right, over the crossroads by the pub and down the lane opposite. *Yeomans Cottage on the left has a 1637 datestone and mullioned windows.* While the lane runs directly to Hanlith Bridge, more rewarding to shortly turn left on a walled lane, which slowly curves back around to the Malham road on the village edge. Here take a stile on the right, into the field proper and across to a wall-stile. A thin path crosses a large field, swinging left to a stile. This reveals Scalegill Mill ahead. Descend the grassy rake to the entrance (see WALK 4) then double back on its driveway, which in tandem with the River Aire runs along to Hanlith Bridge.

Prominent just opposite is Hanlith Hall, which dates back in parts to 1668. Cross the bridge to a stile and accompany the river downstream. The Aire is close company for a considerable stretch of this parkland country. From a kissing-gate at the end continue grandly through a rushy pasture, and just short of the end take a pair of neighbouring small gates as the path cuts a bend of the river. Follow the wall away, keeping straight on when it leaves you, to pass a fence corner leading to a small footbridge. Whilst this also leads to Airton Bridge, opt instead for turning right to a larger footbridge over the Aire itself. Cross it and fork left to a stile in the wall downstream. Beyond a kissing-gate continue on to the start of the old mill-race at another footbridge at the old weir.

The path is now sandwiched between mill-race and river, remaining so to wind round to Airton Mill. *The walk alongside the leat is an interesting mini-history trail, largely dry but still marshy, and with evidence of old workings. The imposing mill, which once spun cotton, is well preserved after conversion into individual flats.* Pass round to the right, into the car park and out onto a road. The bridge is just down to the left, and the green just up to the right. *Returning to the green, a cottage on the right bears a 1696 datestone, and many dovecotes in its central gable, while on the left is the Friends' Meeting House dated 1700.*

The Squatter's House, Airton

13

BELL BUSK

START Airton   Grid ref. SD 902591

DISTANCE 5 miles (8km)

ORDNANCE SURVEY MAPS
1:50,000
Landranger 103 - Blackburn & Burnley
1:25,000
Explorer OL2 - Yorkshire Dales South/West

ACCESS Start from the village centre. Roadside parking, don't impinge upon the green. Served by Skipton-Malham bus.

Easy rambling by riverbank and old lane, plus a great viewpoint

Airton is a tidy village with many old houses tucked away, and several 17th century datestones in evidence. Main feature is the triangular green on which stands the 'squatter's house': in times past this would be home to a local unfortunate, previously of no fixed abode, who had fallen lucky with the powers-that-be. Alongside are the stone posts of the former village stocks. On the northern edge of the village is 17th century Scosthrop Manor.

Leave the green by the telephone box at the south-west corner, crossing over the main road and up the road opposite, signed to Hellifield. *This attractive corner is Town End - note the old water pump by the roadside just past Manor Farm.* Turn off at the first opportunity along a road to the left (signposted Bell Busk). This is also soon forsaken, this time along Kirk Syke Lane to the right. *This farm track is followed throughout its entire length, enjoying views over its hedgerows to the Barden Moor edges and Flasby Fell.* It runs straight on past the farm at Kirk Syke, and on to a grouping of its barns.

A brief change of character sees it become a green way before emerging into a field. Keep straight on a part sunken way, passing an old quarry and a barn to an open field. Advance to a gate ahead, with the fence switching to the left to reach the next gate, in a wall. Follow a fence down to a prominent barn, behind which is a bridge over Otterburn Beck. From it a clear track leads through unkempt surrounds past barns onto a road in Bell Busk. *On the right is Raven Flatts, a fine 17th century house with mullioned windows. Bell Busk's scattered community stands at the confluence of Otterburn Beck with the Aire, and is dominated by the railway. A century ago there were mills spinning silk here. Bell Busk's seven-arch viaduct is a low structure spanning the Aire on the Leeds-Morecambe line.*

Turn left along the road. *On the grassy sward is a slim, free-standing boundary stone, inscribed 'K' (Kirkby Malham) and 'G' (Gargrave).* At the junction cross the road bridge over the beck and fork right immediately on a lesser lane to cross a bridge over the Aire. Haw Crag awaits directly above. The lane heads uphill, now a rougher surface. *Over to the right the viaduct is revealed.* On levelling out you pass an isolated house, and at a farm drive the way becomes rougher, turning sharp left to climb again.

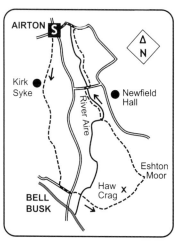

Leave the lane at the next sharp bend right, taking the gate directly ahead to enter the pasture containing Haw Crag. A faint green trackway rises through a gate and up the slope to fade on the edge of the old quarry. The path continues along the fence-side to the gate at the end. *Across the rim of the quarry stands an Ordnance Survey column marking the highest point. Haw Crag's dramatic appearance was enhanced by quarrying a century ago, and the trig. point stands at 676ft/206m atop the steep drop. The*

splendid panorama includes Fountains Fell and Great Whernside beyond the Malhamdale scene, while more distantly the Bowland moors, Pendle Hill and the South Pennines are well represented.

The corner gate, meanwhile, has a stile alongside. Cross the field centre to a faint crossroads with the Pennine Way, which will lead back to Airton. *This area known as Eshton Moor has long since lost any claim to such description.* Take the left branch down to a gate at the bottom of the field, then follow the wall down until it bends away. Now head straight down the centre of this vast field. Directly ahead, the winding Aire is your target. *The large house in view is Newfield Hall, a Holiday Fellowship centre. Also in view are Calton, behind it, and Airton itself.* As the walls converge alongside a road, this narrow way leads down to a gate on the left, and a small beck leads to a footbridge over the river.

From the bridge follow the riverbank upstream, briefly into an encroaching wood before forging on to Newfield Bridge. A stile to its left empties onto the road. Cross the bridge and take a stile on the left to resume upstream. From a stile by a gate follow the wall straight ahead, nearing the river again at two stiles in quick succession. *At this point the Aire is particularly narrow.* From the second stile leave the river again for a stile in the next wall along, and then head across the large pasture, closing in on the river as Airton Bridge comes into view. A stile admits to the road. *Alongside the bridge is the substantial mill, converted to residential use. Note the bell still in place.* Cross the bridge to climb the road back onto the green. *A cottage on the right bears a*

1696 datestone and numerous dovecotes in its central gable, while on the left is the Friends' Meeting House of 1700.

Newfield Bridge on the River Aire

OTTERBURN MOOR

START *Otterburn*   *Grid ref. SD 883577*

DISTANCE 5³4 *miles (9km)*

ORDNANCE SURVEY MAPS
1:50,000
Landranger 103 - Blackburn & Burnley
1:25,000
Explorer OL2 - Yorkshire Dales South/West **or**
Explorer OL41 - Forest of Bowland & Ribblesdale

ACCESS *Otterburn is equidistant from Airton, Hellifield and Bell Busk. There is room for several cars between beck and buildings just upstream of the bridge, or downstream on the west bank.*

> *An upland ramble with barely any uphill work.*
> *Good views from between rolling green foothills*

Otterburn is a sleepy farming hamlet in a fold of the hills, well off the beaten track and a million miles from Malham. When the local inhabitants set out for church, they took the route you are using as far as Scosthrop Lane. This old way, known for obvious reasons as the Kirk Gait, continues on to Kirkby Malham (see WALK 12). Leave the junction by the bridge along the unsigned lane following Otterburn Beck upstream past farm buildings. Almost immediately it becomes a wide track, and beyond a gate it runs free alongside the beck. *During your acquaintance this lively watercourse performs several modest falls over exposed rock.*

On approaching another gate beneath some trees, leave the beckside track by a gate on the right, and from it head half-left across the field to pick up a grassy track rising towards a line of trees. From there head across to the top side of the small wood

53

in front, then accompany its upper boundary to a gate. Aim straight across the field to a stile in the far corner, ignoring a neighbouring stile in the right-hand wall. Follow this wall away in the same direction as before, and when it parts company continue over the brow of the field. *This modest brow is a super vantage point, with the Barden Moor skyline over to the right featuring prominently, with Rye Loaf Hill and Kirkby Fell ahead, Pendle Hill far behind and the Otterburn Moor landscape just over to the left.* Pick out a ladder-stile in the wall ahead, bearing left towards it to emerge onto Scosthrop Lane. *Here you take leave of the Kirk Gait, which forges straight on over the stile opposite.*

Turn left up the road only as far as a walled farm-road striking off to the left. Its undulating course will lead unerringly to the remote farm buildings at Orms Gill Green. *Secreted in a tree-shrouded hollow, features of interest are the large limekiln by the path, and a surprising waterfall* where the lively beck escapes from confinement under the farm into trees below. Old quarry just above the farm.

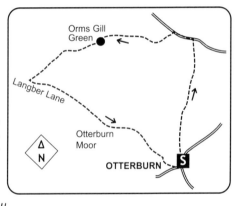

Pass around the back of the farm buildings and remain on the drive up the field behind. As soon as the wall turns away, take a gate in the ensuing fence and bear away from it up to a brow. Forge on ahead to locate a stile in the wall ahead. Continue on a faint trod across an extensive rough pasture, aiming for the bottom of the belt of trees that appears ahead. As you near them tiny Otterburn Beck appears down to the left, and where these two meet, a stile is found in the very corner. From it cross the beck in lovely surroundings and bear right onto the distinct raking path up the slope to your right. At the top it peters out, but a trod runs on past a wall-corner and then slopes down to a stile in the wall ahead. This is one of two walls enclosing the green road of Langber Lane. *This splendid green road runs across the hills towards Settle: your walk makes use of its eastern section. It is joined amid some extensive views to the south-west across the Ribble Valley and down to Pendle Hill and the Bowland moors.*

Turn left along this wide byway, enjoying a short-lived green lane cameo. *Rye Loaf Hill and Kirkby Fell are well seen up to the left.* The lane's demise comes when the right-hand wall parts company. *Ahead is a Barden Moor and Flasby Fell skyline.* Through the gate/stile keep faith with the left-hand wall: though pathless, the hollowed way by the wall confirms its historic nature. Forge on to a gate in a wall at the far end. *From the vicinity of Hellifield Moor Top the extensive panorama includes Rye Loaf Hill, Kirkby Fell, Pikedaw, Malham Moor, Great Whernside, the Cracoe Fell-Crookrise heights, Flasby Fell and Pendle Hill.*

On the other side of the gate a track is picked up coming in from the left, and it takes you down through the pasture to a gate. Running grassily down to a gate at the bottom it enters the edge of Wenningber Plantation, in the care of the Woodland Trust. The track advances on to emerge and descend gently as Dacre Lane back into Otterburn. On reaching the road turn left along it to round a corner with a green and back to the junction by the bridge.

Old limekiln at Orms Gill Green

LANGBER LANE

START *Long Preston*   *Grid ref. SD 834582*

DISTANCE *4³4 miles (7¹2km)*

ORDNANCE SURVEY MAPS
1:50,000
Landranger 103 - Blackburn & Burnley
1:25,000
Explorer OL2 - Yorkshire Dales South/West or
Explorer OL41 - Forest of Bowland & Ribblesdale

ACCESS *Start from the village green outside the Maypole Inn. Parking alongside the green and on the other side of the main road. Skipton-Settle buses pass through, and there is a station on the Leeds-Morecambe/Carlisle line.*

> *A charming little ramble well off the beaten track*

Long Preston is well named, spread along the A65 with its rumble of heavy traffic. It is in fact a very pleasant village that merits more than the second glance it rarely gets. Focal point is the green, graced by a maypole that is annually put to suitable use. Facing it is the appropriately named Maypole Inn, with the Boars Head just along the street. There is also a Post office/store and a tearoom. Strictly, as a Ribblesdale village Long Preston falls outside this book's brief: with partner Hellifield it occupies a no-man's-land, invariably excluded from thoughts of Ribblesdale, which end their interest at Settle. Downstream this no-man's-land extends to the Lancashire border, Gisburn, and the Ribble Valley. However, it has found sanctuary here, and the hinterland you are to explore is firmly attached to the Malhamdale hills, indeed on Langber Lane you can nod at ramblers on WALK 14. What Hellifield does not share with Long Preston is National Park status.

From the back of the green head away along School Lane. Just past a junction behind the school a walled grassy path heads off left. This cuts a corner of the road, but misses out the church. If visiting the church, remain on the narrow lane. *The church gate is to the right, just around the corner. St Mary's church is rather tucked away, but worth a visit. Like its village, it too is long, with a heavy, low-slung roof. Its Norman font has a Jacobean cover, while in the churchyard, near the porch, is a 17th century dated sundial, also bearing many initials, and restored in 1980.*

Leave along the church front to a little gate out of the churchyard back onto New House Lane. *Already you have views over the Ribble Valley to the familiar landmark of Pendle Hill: it will remain in your sights for virtually all the walk.* Quickly picking up the direct route, continue on the downgrading lane. At a fork ignore the

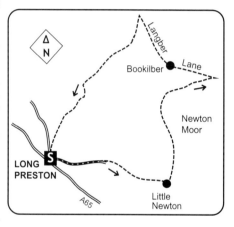

right one which drops to some wooden sheds, whiule the left one leads on through largely more open terrain before rising to end at Little Newton. Keep left of the farm buildings to a set of pens at the end, then take a gate on the left to join the bank of often dry Newton Gill. Within yards a shapely bridge carries you over it and a nice grassy track accompanies it upstream. It fades at Waterfall Rock, where exposed tilted rock strata overlook a hollow above a minor waterfall. Just beyond, a stile admits to a corner of Newton Moor.

Resume upstream, the most used route being a little path dropping to shadow the meandering beck. A higher level trod runs on from above the stile. As the slopes open out rise up a little, only a faintest of trod is traceable across the rough moor-grass. *Over to the left is a nice glimpse of Bowland, with Whelp Stone Crag prominent.* Curve around level ground above a confluence and wall corner, with the beck and parallel wall over to the left, to reach a junction with the next wall ahead. Down to the left a stile and tiny footbridge are not seen until the last moment. Go briefly left up the wallside to a stile on the brow, then slant right up the vast reedy pasture to approach a wall-corner on the left.

Ahead now to the east is a good prospect of the Crookrise edges on Barden Moor. Ahead also, a ladder-stile onto Langber Lane beckons. *Note the redundant old wall-stile alongside.* Turn left along this old green way, quickly reaching the restored house at Bookilber Barn where the way becomes more firmly surfaced. It continues amiably along past a couple of opportunities to return more directly to the village. *Ahead, the flat top of Ingleborough is briefly revealed, while over to the left is a vast sweep featuring the South Pennines, Weets Hill, Pendle Hill, West Pennine Moors, Grindleton Fell, and the Bowland moors.*

Your time to leave comes when the track winds down above Bookil Gill Beck on the left. Double sharply back, ignoring a ladder-stile to pass through a gate. Just a few yards downstream ford the beck, from where a nice green path heads away. As the beck swings more steeply down to the left, the path contours around through an old wall. Head straight on, past a couple of trees on the brow to descend through succeeding gates in walls and pleasantly down to descend a spur above a confluence in a flat strath. Through a kissing-gate cross to a footbridge on Long Preston Beck, and join a track slanting up the bank to the top of the Woodland Trust's New Pasture Plantation. *Look back up the valley of Long Preston Beck to glimpse the weirdly sculpted limestone tors above Settle.*

Just yards beyond the access stile take another stile to forsake the now walled New Pasture Lane. Aim directly away from the corner, on the brow locating a stile ahead. *The houses of Long Preston are suddenly spread out beneath you, backed by Pendle Hill.* Descend right to another stile, and further obvious stiles lead you on. Diagonally across a couple more fields to a stile beyond a circular pool, two final fields are crossed to find a corner-stile onto Green Gate Lane. Turn left to finish.

CONISTON COLD

START *Gargrave   Grid ref. SD 931541*

DISTANCE *6¹⁄4 miles (10km)*

ORDNANCE SURVEY MAPS
1:50,000
Landranger 103 - Blackburn & Burnley
1:25,000
Explorer OL2 - Yorkshire Dales South/West

ACCESS *Start from the Dalesman Cafe on the main street opposite the bridge. Two car parks on West Street, alongside. Served by Skipton-Settle bus and by Leeds-Morecambe/Carlisle trains.*

An unassuming ramble to a couple of small settlements linked by good paths and tracks, culminating on the canal towpath

For a note on Gargrave please see page 62. Leave the main street along West Street, almost opposite the bridge over the Aire, and at the second car park bear left over Higherland Bridge alongside a lock on the canal. At the junction beyond keep left on Mark House Lane which winds along before turning right to rise gradually away alongside a wood. *For a simpler start remain on this old packhorse way which becomes a good cart track all the way to Bell Busk.*

Part way up leave by a gate on the left, from where a broad, embanked path drops down to a gate in a fence. Through it turn right with the fence to a wall-stile at the end, and resume with a fence. Keep straight on to merge with the hedge enclosing the lane, rising gently to the brow where bear a little left to a small gate in a wall. Now cross a large field bearing right, again with a fence leading along to the right edge of a domed wood. A spring is passed part way on. From a corner stile advance just as far as the wood end, then use a stile to resume on the other side of the fence. *Opening up ahead are the heights of Rye Loaf Hill, Kirkby Fell and the more distant Fountains Fell.* Towards the end bear left to a wall-stile ahead and cross to another in a tiny section of wall. *Bell Busk appears below, with longer views to Pendle Hill over to the left.* Now slant left down this large field, close by a wall corner and down to a gate in the far corner. This puts you back on Mark House Lane. Turn down it, soon improving its surface to drop down to cross the Aire in Bell Busk.

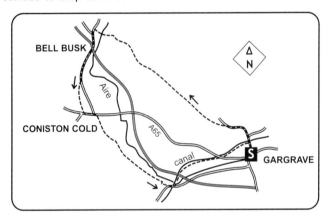

At the road junction turn left to bridge Otterburn Beck, and immediately left again. *The scattered community of Bell Busk is dominated by the railway, and a century ago mills spun silk here.* This road shadows the beck and its imminent confluence with the Aire, out of the village underneath the viaduct. *Bell Busk's seven-arch viaduct is a low structure spanning the Aire on the Leeds-Morecambe line.* Keep on until the road starts to climb. At this point take a gate on the right and slant up the field past a plantation corner and across to a gate in the fence. Coniston Cold's isolated church is seen across to the left. *The gate is shared with a flagged churchgoers' path leading from unseen Coniston Hall.* Rise left with the fence over a brow and along to a drive, crossing it to a stile and cross a small field to a wall-stile by a gate onto the busy A65 in the tiny village of Coniston Cold. Cross with care and go left along the footway. *An old guidestone at the junction is inscribed Settle and Bell Busk.*

Opposite the side road turn right along a driveway, which swings left to emerge via a cattle-grid into a field. When this swings uphill take a kissing-gate in front, and advance along two nice fieldsides to a gate at the end. Cross a field centre to a wall-stile, then drop left to a stile in a marshy corner above a pond, with the Aire just below. Rise left to pass round the left side of a plantation, then on past it to a brow. *This reveals the canal aqueduct over the Aire, backed by Pinhaw, northernmost limit of the South Pennine moors: looking back are Rye Loaf Hill and Kirkby Fell.* Drop straight down to a gate in a fence below, then bear left to an ox-bow on the Aire, a pleasant spot. Now cross to the nearby fence to find a stile in it where a wall adjoins. Go left along the fieldside to a gate at the end onto a back road.

Cross Priest Holme Bridge and then double back underneath it onto the towpath of the Leeds-Liverpool Canal. *The bank offers immediate interest, first in the aqueduct above the River Aire, then straight under the railway, with its viaduct over the river visible just down-*

stream. The final section sees Gargrave's scattered locks begin, the third being alongside the Anchor Inn. All day refreshments and a large outdoor area and play-ground may well divert attention. Happily the canal then takes you under the main road, to conclude round the back of the village. At the road bridge at Higherland Lock (old milestone: Liverpool 93, Leeds $34^{1}4$), abandon the towpath and turn down the lane to re-enter the village alongside the main car park.

Old guidepost, Coniston Cold

AROUND ESHTON

START *Gargrave   Grid ref. SD 931541*

DISTANCE *5^{3}4 miles (9km)*

ORDNANCE SURVEY MAPS
1:50,000
Landranger 103 - Blackburn & Burnley
1:25,000
Explorer OL2 - Yorkshire Dales South/West

ACCESS *Start from the Dalesman Cafe on the main street. Two car parks on West Street, alongside. Served by Skipton-Settle bus and by Leeds-Morecambe/Carlisle trains.*

> *Gentle walking around the scattered charms of Eshton*

Gargrave is an attractive village that makes an ideal base for Malhamdale. Although Skipton, main centre for the southern Dales, is only 10 minutes distant by road, here is a more intimate Dales atmosphere. The village is split by the busy A65 running through it: lined by shops, the main street widens into a spacious area by the war memorial, where a sturdy bridge crosses the Aire to the parish church. Dedicated to St Andrew, it was restored in 1852: the tower dates from the early 16th century.

The Pennine Way passes through the village, and the two central pubs, the Old Swan and the Masons Arms, provide lunchtime breaks for those midway between Earby and Malham. The Leeds-Liverpool Canal also comes this way, reaching the northernmost point of its 127^{1}4 miles as it meets the National Park boundary. The waterway takes advantage of the Aire Gap to squeeze through the Pennines, and a third pub, the Anchor, stands alongside.

From Gargrave to Haw Crag your route follows that of the Pennine Way, 70 miles into its total of 270 and at the very out-set of its 53 miles in the Yorkshire Dales National Park. Leave the main street along West Street, almost opposite the bridge over the Aire, and at the second car park bear left over Higherland Bridge alongside a lock on the canal. At the junction beyond keep left on Mark House Lane which becomes a leafy byway rising gradually away. After the demise of the trees on the right, take a stile into the field on the same side. *The former packhorse way, meanwhile, continues to Bell Busk.*

Though still on the Pennine Way, its presence is far less obvious now. Remain parallel with the lane for a short distance, then strike across the field to a stile in the fence ahead. Advance to the near corner then slant steeply up to a stile above. Continue the climb to the top corner of the planta-tion on Harrows Hill. *Over to the right are Cracoe Fell, Flasby Fell and Skipton Moor, with Pendle Hill behind you.*

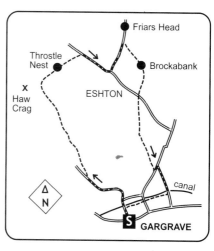

Ignore a gate in the fence ahead in favour of a kissing-gate along to the left, from where strike diagonally across the field to another. Maintain this course to the wall ahead, and follow it left to a gate in the very corner. From it head off directly over the brow of the field. Descend part way down the field centre, noting a gate/stile in the wall to the left. This sends an invisible path across to form a crossroads with the Pennine Way, which you are about to leave. Turn sharp right and head for the faint glimpse of the farm at Throstle Nest. *At this stage you can savour a fine aspect northwards to the Malhamdale scene.* Cross straight over a permanent track and advance to the edge of the field, the farm appearing down to the left. Your way bears a little right to a small gate at the near edge of a small plantation. Slant down outside the trees to a gate/stile below, over a farm track, and away along the wallside to join the farm drive. Advance along this pleasant course out onto a road. *The drive is a fine vantage point for enjoying the prospect of the Barden Moor massif and the shapely tops of Flasby Fell, straight ahead.*

Turn right to descend to the junction at Eshton. *This is the Malham road, which can be busy on summer weekends - take care. At the junction admire the lovely house of St Helens: it has five bays and dates from the 18th century. Eshton is a scattered community with no definable centre. It has several other fine buildings, including Eshton House also by this junction, and the Hall, dating from 1827 and now a residential home on the road towards Gargrave.* Escape left along the quiet back road towards Winterburn. *Note a sundial on St Helens' garage.*

The lane runs on past St Helen's Well, in a wooded corner on the left as the road runs down to the bridge on Eshton Beck. *It was clearly given greater respect in times past, when local people would have placed faith in its healing properties. Nevertheless today it remains a pleasing sight when the water gurgles up into a part man-made pool. Ahead now the engaging prospect of Friars Head is revealed further along the road. This superb 17th century house is the most interesting in the district and looks entirely lost in this rural setting. Its south front is a remarkably intricate four bayed labyrinth of mullioned windows. The monks of Furness Abbey had a grange here, and farm life survives.*

Before Friars Head, however, on a bend after the bridge, double back right on a wallside track. This runs on beneath a wood covering an old quarry to fade at a wall corner. Cross to the wall corner opposite, and rise outside the wooded confines of the beck to run along to Brockabank. *Before reaching it, look back to see a splendid old limekiln at the edge of the wood.* Take a stile by the gate in the very corner, from where a green way passes beneath the front of the house. *With mullioned windows and exquisite location this is a beautiful old place dating back to the 17th century. Down below, the wooded environs of the beck further contribute to the charms of this lovely corner.*

The drive is joined and leads quickly down to the arch of Brockabank Bridge. *To the left through the trees is an extensive old quarry face, with another limekiln just below.* Part way up the other side, on a slight bend, take a stile and slant up the field brow on the left to the top corner of a plantation. Here bear right alongside Eshton Grange to a stile back onto the road.

Cross to one almost opposite and head away, reaching a stile in the adjacent fence just short of the end. A path crosses the field to another stile and along to an old iron kissing-gate into the trees. A good path heads away, passing a remote dwelling before emerging into a large field. *The delightful parkland hereabouts is part of the former park of Eshton Hall.* Slant left down to an iron stile and maintain the same course with a line of stately trees to a wall-stile onto a road on the edge of the village. Either double back to a junction and turn right as far as Ray Bridge on the canal, or simply keep straight along the footway into Gargrave. Either leads to a short towpath walk (right) back to the canal crossing near the start of the walk. *Ray Bridge, incidentally, marks the northernmost point of the Leeds-Liverpool Canal.*

Friars Head

EAST MARTON

START *Gargrave   Grid ref. SD 931541*

DISTANCE *6^{1}2 miles (10^{1}2km)*

ORDNANCE SURVEY MAPS
1:50,000
Landranger 103 - Blackburn & Burnley
1:25,000
Explorer OL2 - Yorkshire Dales South/West

ACCESS *Start from the bridge in the village centre. Two car parks on West Street, across the main road. Served by Skipton-Settle bus and by Leeds-Morecambe/Carlisle trains.*

> *This rural ramble is dominated by a towpath trod that exhibits a remarkable variety of interest*

For a note on Gargrave please see page 62. Cross the bridge over the Aire in the village centre and turn immediately right on the path upstream. This runs past several houses and alongside a former mill-cut, to leave the riverside green at a corner and emerge onto a street. Turn left to join Marton Road. Go briefly right, then left on an enclosed drive serving Scaleber Farm. This runs for some time largely between hedgerows and bridging the railway line. *At this point the route of the Pennine Way joins in, and remains your way to the canal at East Marton.*

After climbing to a cattle-grid, turn off the drive at a stile on the left and bear gently away up the field. A track comes up from the right but you soon cross it at right-angles to rise to an old stake on the brow. *Here you have a fair prospect ahead, to Pendle Hill dominating the scene. Back over your left shoulder are the heights of Flasby Fell, backed by the higher*

Cracoe Fell with its monument prominent. To the right are the Malhamdale heights of Rye Loaf Hill and Kirkby Fell leading the eye to the very beginnings of the Aire.

With Pendle Hill as a guide, advance to a kissing-gate then head away with a fence to a stile at the end. Bear left over the field to the next corner stile, then head away with the fence again. From the next stile drop to a stile by a gate over the tiny Crickle Beck. Now bear right, a short way from the fence shadowing the stream, and on through an intervening gate and on again to a fence-end adjacent to a farm bridge by a modern barn. With a sliver of wood-

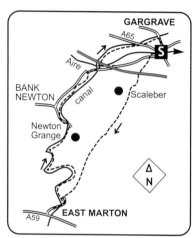

land to the right, advance straight on again to a stile, and through several more in quick succession, closing in on the tree-lined trickle to drop to a stile in the adjacent hedge. This sees you cross the stream on a plank footbridge. Across, bear left up the field to reach a wall-stile in the far bottom corner, joining a rough lane. *For a short-cut, turn right here until picking up the main route on the canal bank.*

Turn left along the lane and after 200 yards take a stile on the left. This short section short-cuts a large bend in the lane. Cross the field to a stile on the left of the wood ahead, from where a short-lived walled way rises alongside the trees. A novel stile at the top sees you back out. Through a small gate a thin path ascends the field, bearing away from the wood (enclosing a long-abandoned quarry) to cross to a slim stile at the far corner. This admits to the now surfaced lane. Follow it left past further recolonised quarries, quickly reaching Williamson Bridge on the canal at East Marton.

There are always plenty of boats moored here, while just ahead, the A59 is seen crossing the canal by a vertically double-arched bridge. The reason for this strange arrangement is simply the busy nature of the road: the older, lower arch has long been superseded by the need for the sturdier, higher one.

Your return route takes to the towpath here, but the few attractions of the hamlet may first merit attention.

Continuing straight over the bridge, some attractive housing is passed - that to the right sporting mullioned windows, including some arched-headed, and alongside is a licensed tearoom. Just up the lane, alongside the main road, is the popular Cross Keys pub and a small green. The parish church is somewhat out of the way on the other side of the A59.

Free-standing pub sign at East Marton

Back at the canal, double back under Williamson Bridge to commence the return. Here the route description comes to an end, for though the walk is not yet halfway through, all that remains is to follow the waterway back to Gargrave. *Its various meanderings ensure that this is a longer return, especially in the early stages: a glance at the map confirms the canal's dogged attempts to maintain its contour result in a right old weaving about. This section has a curiously remote feeling to it, and remains entirely grassy. Increasingly, Flasby Fell forms a colourful backdrop, flanked by Cracoe Fell to one side and Embsay Crag on the other.*

Approaching Bank Newton an old milestone features the waterway's extremities - Liverpool 91, Leeds 36¼. The old lane is then briefly rejoined before it crosses the canal. Here double back under the road bridge to regain the towpath just short of the first of Bank Newton's locks. *There now follows a splendid string of such locks, seven in all. This section is full of interest, and summer weekends are likely to see much activity by the boating fraternity. An old canal house at Legaston Bank bears a 1791 datestone.*

The moorings follow the locks, beyond which another short road section is forced until the next bridge. *Doubling back underneath Priest Holme Bridge, the bank offers immediate further interest, first in an aqueduct above the River Aire, then straight under the railway, with its viaduct over the river just downstream. The final section sees Gargrave's scattered locks begin, the third being alongside the Anchor Inn. All day refreshments and a large outdoor area and playground may well divert attention. Happily the canal then takes you under the main road, to conclude round the back of the village.* At the road bridge at Higherland Lock (milestone: Liverpool 93, Leeds 34¼), finally abandon the towpath and turn down the road to re-enter the village alongside the main car park.

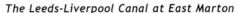

The Leeds-Liverpool Canal at East Marton

WINTERBURN VALLEY

START *Winterburn*   *Grid ref. SD 935586*

DISTANCE *6^{1}4 miles (10km)*

ORDNANCE SURVEY MAPS
1:50,000
Landranger 98 - Wensleydale & Upper Wharfedale
Landranger 103 - Blackburn & Burnley
1:25,000
Explorer OL2 - Yorkshire Dales South/West

ACCESS *Start from the road junction in the hamlet. Parking on or just off the Hetton-Airton road skirting the hamlet.*

An easy circuit of a lovely lake, returning via a fine old house

Winterburn is a small farming community set in an attractive fold of the hills. Here is a former chapel of 1703, one of the first Independent chapels. Restored early last century, as Chapel House it is now a private residence. From the T-junction head along the dead-end road through the heart of the hamlet, passing the venerable Rookery Farm on the right. At a cattle-grid it becomes a private farm road, crossing a length of pasture by the beck to arrive at a bridge. Across it follow the road along to the right, a lovely stroll through woodland still alongside the beck. After a time it gradually climbs above the beck to approach the old reservoir keeper's house, with the grassy dam of Winterburn Reservoir ahead. Your route however does not quite reach the house, instead turn sharp left up the drive that leads circuitously but unerringly to Way Gill Farm. *Views open out beyond a first glimpse of the reservoir to Cracoe Fell and Crookrise Crag, also out to Flasby Fell and Pendle Hill.*

Without entering its yard cross the field to a gate to the right of the house. Bear gently left down the field, with Winterburn Reservoir now laid out ahead. At the bottom a stile admits onto another farm road. This goes left to High Cow House, but you leave it before the farm, at a wall-stile on the right. Head down the fieldside to approach the reservoir. At the bottom turn left for a delightful ramble alongside the shore, and on through several fields above the upper reach of the reservoir, to reach a stone arched bridge over Bordley Beck before it enters the lake. *Beneath a fence shortly before it, a stone inscribed LLC indicates that the reservoir was constructed to supply the Leeds-Liverpool Canal at Gargrave.*

The reservoir at Winterburn is a substantial finger-like sheet of water, and at times could easily be mistaken for being natural. Even the dam with its grass cover seems to blend in: the old keeper's house has been restored. A variety of birdlife takes advantage of this peaceful setting. The Winterburn Valley is split into two very different sections by the reservoir: downstream is a deep, heavily-wooded confine, while the head of the lake points to more extensive, moor-like terrain.

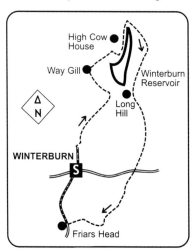

Across the bridge is a large expanse of rough pasture, and a firmly surfaced bridlepath heads up it, briefly half-left before turning right to rise gradually. *Ever broadening views over the reservoir are backed by a distant but prominent Pendle Hill.* The path slowly levels out to arrive at a gate in a descending wall at the head of the unsurfaced Moor Lane. *At this Piccadilly Circus of footpaths a guidepost points in no less than five directions, to Bordley, Hetton, Threshfield, Winterburn and Malham. Don't go astray here!*

Pass through the gate then leave immediately by a gate on the right. Cross a rough pasture to a conspicuous gap in the belt of trees at Alans Plantation ahead. Re-emerging, a thin path (aided by stakes) heads across an immense tract of rough pasture towards a cluster of trees surrounding Long Hill Farm. *Now you have a good prospect of the wooded lower valley, along with Cracoe and Flasby Fells, the South Pennines, Pendle Hill, Grindleton Fell and the Bowland moors.* Through a gate in a fence converge with a wall on the right, passing outside the farming confines and on to a corner gate. Advance on the fieldside past a barn conversion to the next corner gate, with a wall-stile alongside.

Entering a large domed pasture head diagonally away, a thin but clear grassy trod curving round to the left of the brow of the field with the graceful peak of Sharp Haw as an approximate guide. *The Barden Moor edges look superb across to the left.* Dropping down to the far corner, use a gate a few yards to the right. Head directly away to join a wall on your left, passing two barns at Owslin Laithe and remaining on this grassy wallside path through one further field to emerge onto the crest of the Hetton-Winterburn road.

Cross to a gate opposite and head down with the wall to a gate/stile in the corner, then continue on a pleasant little wallside path (rising past the barn of Scarnber Laithe) to eventually reach a gate at the far end. Head away again with the wall now on the right, as far as a gate in a fence just ahead (this differs from the map). *Enjoy a closing look back at the rugged skyline from Cracoe Fell to Flasby Fell as the Malhamdale hills of Rye Loaf Hill and Kirkby Fell appear ahead.* From the gate bear right on a faint path to drop to merge with a wall to the right. Ignore the gate in it and continue down the wallside to a corner gate. Now simply accompany the wall on the right down through further fields to a gate onto Winterburn Lane opposite Friars Head.

Detour left a few yards to appraise the house itself. *This superb 17th century house is the most interesting in the district, and looks entirely lost in this remote setting. Its south front is a remarkably intricate four-bayed facade of mullioned windows. The monks of Furness Abbey had a grange here, and farm life survives (Illustrated on page 65).* Turn right along the quiet road for a short walk back into Winterburn.

BORDLEY

START Boss Moor   Grid ref. SD 955619

DISTANCE 5¹2 miles (9km)

ORDNANCE SURVEY MAPS
1:50,000
Landranger 98 - Wensleydale & Upper Wharfedale
1:25,000
Explorer OL2 - Yorkshire Dales South/West

ACCESS To reach Boss Moor first go to Hetton. From the bus shelter at the Rylstone junction take the Cracoe road, and after 100 yards Fleets Lane forks left (Bordley 4). Halfway up it emerges onto open moor. On the brow ahead is a parking place on the right, with an old quarry in close proximity.

A fine combination of unfrequented valley and moorland walking

Before starting glance over the wall for a most complete view of Winterburn Reservoir, with Pendle Hill behind. The walk commences with a gentle stroll along the road towards Bordley. Ahead are splendid views over the valley you are to explore. The road winds downhill before becoming enclosed to reach the phone box and farm at Lainger. Here take the farm track left, shadowing a beck down past a barn conversion to Bordley Beck in the valley bottom. Immediately across take a stile on the right to follow the beck upstream, over another stile and on to a gate by a few trees.

The deeply confined valley of Bordley Beck is a charming location hidden from the outside world. Its colourful slopes form the Winterburn Valley (see WALK 19). From the gate cross the part reedy pasture above the beck, with the isolated farm of Bordley Hall ahead. Don't return to the beck but bear left to drop to a sidestream, going left a short way to a wall-stile across it. Head away with the wall, merging into a track to reach a wall-corner level with the farm. There is a bubbling spring here.

Turn right with the track to a gate behind the buildings, then left to a gate just above. Now climb the large, steep field to a gate only revealed near the top. *Pause here to savour grand views back down the valley.* With the gradient easing bear right to locate a stile hidden near a corner. The limestone country now dominates all around you. Advancing from the stile a farm track is soon joined heading for Bordley, which quickly appears just ahead. It is entered between farm buildings directly across the

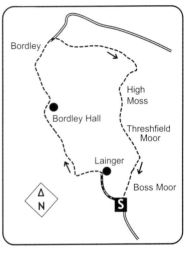

last smaller field. *Bordley is a farming hamlet standing at a breezy near-1100 feet above sea level. Its remoteness is stressed by the fact that several lanes head towards it, but none actually reach it as fully made up roads. A plethora of footpaths and bridleways radiate from the centre. The solid stone buildings are spread around a large green, workmanlike rather than picturesque. The hamlet shelters from the weather's worst extremes by virtue of its position in a hollow.*

Turn right through the hamlet, departing on the surfaced road at the other end. Quickly climbing to a gate where it becomes unenclosed, turn immediately right to run above a wall. *Looking ahead to the nick through which the path runs, note the remarkable contrast formed by the presence of the Craven Fault, with gleaming limestone to the left and gritstone country to the right.* As the wall falls away forge on to drop to a stile at a second wall junction in the dip just ahead. From it a thin wallside path makes the short steep pull opposite. As the wall turns off at the brow a grassy track comes in from the left at a spring with a pair of stone troughs to forge straight on. *Look back to see Bordley's fine setting.*

The path maintains a straight line beneath limestone scars high to the left, and soon encounters a battery of stiles set in successive walls. From the last one the little path aims straight ahead towards a barn in the corner. *Note the tiny beck disappearing at Higher Height Holes on the right, and a splendidly preserved limekiln to the left.* A fine wall-stile deposits you onto an enclosed grassy track above the barn of Height Laithe. *Ahead is Simon's Seat across Wharfedale, with the great mass of Barden Moor closer right; note also, much nearer, the black entrances to Calf Hole (or Height Cave), which has revealed evidence of Bronze Age and Iron Age occupation.* Turn right along the short enclosed way to a pair of gates at the far end. From it a firm bridle-track heads away across the moorland of High Moss, rising to a gate in a fence. *Pause to look back over the last stage, and to see the broad shoulders of Great Whernside further up Wharfedale.*

The track continues across open moor, and soon after reaching a wall you are channeled through a pleasant walled way onto Threshfield Moor. The track remains with the right-hand wall as far as a bridleway junction at a gate onto Boss Moor. Pass through and a good grassy track heads diagonally away. *This glorious return features Barden Moor, Flasby Fell, the South Pennines, Pendle Hill and Bowland within its panorama.* With the Bordley lane soon in view, your improving track avoids it until reaching the old quarries and the car.

A corner of Bordley

RYLSTONE EDGES

START *Rylstone*   *Grid ref. SD 969586*

DISTANCE *6 miles (9^{1}2km)*

ORDNANCE SURVEY MAPS
1:50,000
Landranger 103 - Blackburn & Burnley
1:25,000
Explorer OL2 - Yorkshire Dales South/West

ACCESS *Start from the pond alongside the main road. Parking alongside, and also just along the road north at a lay-by. Served by Skipton-Grassington bus. •OPEN ACCESS: see page 6.*

A memorable moorland stroll linking two celebrated gritstone edge landmarks, enjoying a good dose of history and big views

Rylstone is a tiny village but full of interest, with its attractive roadside pond fringed by springtime daffodils. Near St Peter's church was the home of the Norton family who took part in 1536 in the Pilgrimage of Grace, and three years later the Rising of the North. Their unfortunate story is recounted by Wordsworth in his 'The White Doe of Rylstone'. Much more recently Rylstone shot to fame as its Womens' Institute became the celebrated 'Calendar Girls', whose remarkable story is surely known to all. There is an old milestone on the junction across from the pond, while from the outset both Rylstone Cross and the Cracoe Fell obelisk wait high above.

From the pond, cross the road with care and head up the lane opposite. Passing the Manor House on the right, it leads to the church. Just beyond, turn sharp right on a rough, initially enclosed track. At the far corner of the field it continues along a wallside and then on into an open field. *Rylstone Cross and the Cracoe Fell obelisk provide prominent and arresting objectives high on the moorland skyline.* At a pocket of trees the track swings sharp right and drops down through a couple of gates onto a walled rough lane. Turn left along this for a few minutes, and as it starts to rise away take a gate on the left alongside an information board. This is the entry point for a concession path leading to the access area.

A good track crosses the reedy pasture, climbing steeply past a plantation and up to a gate fronting the access area. The track now ascends through some dense bracken with newly planted trees on the left. As the track starts to level out a green way heads off left with the fence. This quickly rises to a stile in it, from where a thinner path slants up out of the bracken to run beneath the tumble of rocks above. It

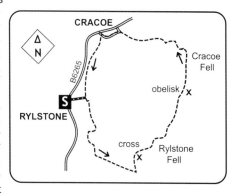

soon reaches a ladder-stile at a wall-corner. Over the wall is the heathery expanse of the heart of the moor. For now follow the wall away, enjoying sweeping views to quickly reach Rylstone Cross.

Rylstone Cross crowns a natural gritstone base. Erected to celebrate the Paris treaty of 1813, it is a prominent landmark from the road below. On view are Rye Loaf Hill, Kirkby Fell, Ingleborough, Fountains Fell, Birks Fell, Yockenthwaite Moor, Buckden Pike and Great Whernside. In the winter of 1992/1993 the old stone shaft with its wooden arms succumbed to severe gales, and was replaced in the spring of 1995.

The Cracoe Fell obelisk is the next objective, and there are two ways of reaching it. The traditional walk is along the moor-side of the wall. Cross this by the nearby ladder-stile and head off on a well-worn path, which undulates (passing a Rylstone/Cracoe boundary stone) but gradually climbs the extra 330ft/100m to reach another stile giving access to the obelisk. *More intrepid walkers will remain on the near side of the wall. This thinner path enjoys superior views and more rugged surrounds, in place of the equally grand moorland atmosphere. Of several groups of rocks hogging the edge, the second one demands a modest scramble to descend through, or an alternative descent to pass beneath the rocks. The outcrops supporting the cross and the group beyond offer superb gritstone climbs. Yorkshire classics such as 'President's Slab' and 'Dental Slab' are among well over a hundred named routes on these crags, which are sufficiently high and remote to attract only those climbers able to fellwalk. Eventually, beyond a monster rock, the wall curves around to a ladder-stile at a junction. Cross it and make the short climb to the obelisk, largely on a splendid green hollowed way.*

Cracoe's memorial to its war dead is an even greater landmark than Rylstone Cross. Looking out over this green and pleasant land (quarries excluded), it is a poignant reminder of what our forebears - many who would barely have been out of their own village until then - sacrificed for what we enjoy today. The solid structure is made of the same rock on which it is perched, and not surprisingly commands a glorious view. Its moor-edge location ensures that the distant Dales mountains featured from Rylstone Cross are complemented by a richer collection of village clusters such as Hetton, Threshfield and Grassington.

From the obelisk the next objective is Fell Lane climbing out of Cracoe. It will be seen just to the right of the village at the foot of the moor. Whilst a direct descent is possible, a nicer option awaits. A level path heads away from the obelisk, parallel with the wall over to the right. After about 150 yards fork left, and the way winds distinctly around to approach the scant remains of a basic stone shelter. Just beneath this the way becomes immediately unmistakable as it commences a splendid slant down the fellside. *These innumerable braided ways are old sledgates, worn deep by the passage of sledges loaded with quarried stone, and long since grassed over. Throughout this the views are quite magnificent.*

This great groove absorbs several other such tracks, and just below a lower junction a small cairn suggests a slim, steeper path straight down towards the reedy moor foot. The sunken way, meanwhile, eventually doubles back to falter in the same reedy ground before the bottom wall. The intake gate is just along to the left, defended by sheep pens. The lane is a splendid green way in its first half before the addition of a farm track. At a cottage it becomes surfaced, and just before reaching the main road there is a chance to avoid it. Turn left along a narrow lane, right at the end, then sharp left again as it runs behind the Devonshire Arms. *The little settlement of Cracoe marks the barely discernible watershed between Airedale and Wharfedale. Its long, low pub has a good few years' history behind it, and like several others in the district it bears the arms of the family whose moor you have just been tramping. There is also a very popular cafe next door, and a farm shop and tearoom over the road.*

Unless seeking refreshment keep straight on, with the charming company of a little stream for a while before leaving the village behind. On reaching the main road, don't join it but turn left up the walled trackway of historic Chapel Lane. This quickly levels out and runs a pleasant course back to Rylstone. *Towards the end note the base of a former wayside cross.* Further, the now re-inforced track enters a field ahead. Advance along the wallside to Manor House Farm. *Grassy banks on the left still support ancient fishponds, with your cirque of fells as a superb final backdrop.* From a gate at the end the lane-head at the start of the walk is rejoined. Follow the lane back past the church to finish.

Cracoe Fell from Rylstone Fell

22

FLASBY FELL

START *Rylstone   Grid ref. SD 969586*

DISTANCE *6 miles (9$\frac{1}{2}$km)*

ORDNANCE SURVEY MAPS
1:50,000
Landranger 103 - Blackburn & Burnley
1:25,000
Explorer OL2 - Yorkshire Dales South/West

ACCESS *Start from the pond alongside the main road. Parking alongside, and also just along the road north at a lay-by. Served by Skipton-Grassington bus. •OPEN ACCESS: see page 6.*

> *A landmark fell is sandwiched between charming beckside and field walking on this superbly varied walk*

Rylstone is a tiny village but full of interest, with its attractive roadside pond fringed by springtime daffodils. Near St Peter's church was the home of the Norton family who took part in 1536 in the Pilgrimage of Grace, and three years later the Rising of the North. Their unfortunate story is recounted by Wordsworth in his 'The White Doe of Rylstone'. Much more recently Rylstone shot to fame as its Womens' Institute became the celebrated 'Calendar Girls', whose remarkable story is surely known to all. There is an old milestone on the junction across from the pond, while both Rylstone Cross and the Cracoe Fell obelisk occupy the moorland skyline high above.

From the pond head briefly along the road leaving the main road, but before the railway bridge turn left along a side road. This winds round to end at a farm, where turn right along an enclosed rough lane. At the end it swings left to a gate into a field, then turns right. Through another gate the track fades, simply keep straight on the fieldside to find a wall-stile in the corner alongside High Croft Plantation. *Across to your right is Hetton, by which you will return. Across the stile Flasby Fell reveals itself, though Sharp Haw remains hidden until intervening Rough Haw is surmounted.* Bear left down the field, soon locating an underpass beneath the railway line. *This mineral line serves the massive Swinden limestone quarry beyond Cracoe. It originally ran to Threshfield, for Grassington, but long since lost its passenger service.* Drop left to a footbridge on Calton Gill Beck, with a stile behind. Ascend the field, passing a pair of lone trees and aiming left of the skyline Hull Gap Plantation. *Over to your left Cracoe and Rylstone edges form an arresting skyline.* From the wall corner go to a corner just behind, and from the gate there cross a slimmer field to a gate onto the foot of Flasby Fell.

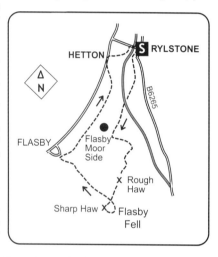

You are now on Open Access land, with the farm of Flasby Moor Side just to the right. Rise onto a firm track and go left with it, a pleasant, improving course around the northern base of the fell. Curving up around Ten Acre Plantation, Rough Haw returns to view. At the track's high point bear left across a neck of land to double back up with an old sunken way to an arrangement of gates in the wall. The path then rises left and fades as it points to a prominent gate in the next wall. Now on the slopes of Rough Haw, easiest way to the top is to squeeze through bracken up the wall-side, then bear left for a steep pull through boulders onto the upper reaches. A thin trod runs by scattered rocks to reveal the sturdy cairn just ahead. Only now does your ultimate goal of Sharp

Haw enter the scene. *Not looking too sharp from this angle, its OS column is prominent.* At 1112ft/339m Rough Haw is secondary to its neighbour, but is a grand top with a sunken walled shelter.

A clear path heads for Sharp Haw, quickly dropping towards the depression separating the two. Keep right at an early fork and the path rapidly drops down through scattered rocks to where a bridle-gate awaits in the wall. You shall return to this point after the short loop around Sharp Haw. A broad path rises from the gate and can be traced all the way up, but as this is your return route, better to take the bridleway's left fork halfway up, crossing to a gate in the wall there. Through this turn up the steepening wallside to meet another path under the very summit of the fell. A welcome seat shelters by the wall, and an old iron stile admits to the Ordnance Survey column on Sharp Haw's airy crest.

Descending Sharp Haw, looking over Rough Haw to Cracoe Fell

At 1171ft/357m Sharp Haw is the highest point of Flasby Fell, this large triangle of upland between Skipton, Gargrave and Rylstone. Ably supported by Rough Haw it is a familiar sight to travellers approaching Skipton up the Aire Valley, and the pairing have always been the author's 'gateway' to the Dales. Though close neighbours, these colourful tops are anything but twins: their titles are apt enough description. The splendid panorama includes Skipton town, the Aire Valley, the South Pennines, Pendle Hill, the Bowland moors, Rye Loaf Hill, Kirkby Fell, Fountains Fell, Great Whernside and Barden Moor.

Leave by following the path along the short ridge for a few strides, then fork right down through a gateway. The path heads straight down through heather, absorbing the bridleway to return to the gate in the depression. The main path heads left to shortly commence its descent to the top corner of a wood. At times moistly it continues down outside the trees to cross Septeria Gill at the bottom, behind which is a gate in the corner. Leaving the fell advance along the fieldside to a gate from where an enclosed track heads off. Ignoring a cross-track serving a barn, your way winds pleasantly down to the yard of Flasby Hall Farm. *Flasby is a tiny settlement consisting of a few scattered houses and farms: a little further downstream stands Flasby Hall.*

Over the bridge take a gate on the right, and cross a pair of paddocks to the beckside. Follow Flasby Beck upstream, and at a crumbling barn head up the centre of the field on a pronounced embankment, now high above the beck. *The extent of Flasby Fell is well arrayed across the beck.* This runs to the far side, where a fence is joined to lead back down to the beck. Beyond a gate you cross gap-stiles either side of the farm road serving Flasby Moor Side. A vague path runs upstream to a ladder-stile defended by a marsh. Head up the slope behind, and then on through a couple of stiles high above a steep wooded bank. The way ahead is clear to and beyond the next stile, after which the faint path slants down, yet again, to the stream (now known as Hetton Beck) at the far end.

Ignore the footbridge in favour of the ladder-stile in front, and continue on a path upstream to reveal Hetton ahead. Beyond one more stile the path slants up to the left, forsaking the beck to cross to a stile in a facing wall. One last field is crossed to a stile onto the road on the edge of Hetton. *On your left is the stone trough of Tossit Well.* Turn right into the village. *Hetton is an attractive village largely free of tourist crowds, though the Angel Inn attracts diners from far and wide. Among its features are a Wesleyan Chapel of 1859 and an old pinfold beyond the pub.*

The final leg leaves by a path down the side of a barn, at a junction by a small green before reaching the pub. This grand old way zigzags down to the beck again, though at the first bend a stile sees a fieldpath short-cut a corner. Cross the beck in style by a hoary old slab bridge. *Supported by two lesser acolytes, its hollowed centre suggests it has seen the passage of many generations of feet and hooves.* A walled snicket heads up the other side, joining a drive to emerge alongside the railway onto the road. Turn under the bridge to finish.

The pond, Rylstone   *Above: The Angel Inn, Hetton*

23

EMBSAY MOOR

START Embsay   Grid ref. SE 009538

DISTANCE $6^3/4$ miles (11km)

ORDNANCE SURVEY MAPS
1:50,000
Landranger 103 - Blackburn & Burnley
Landranger 104 - Leeds, Bradford & Harrogate
1:25,000
Explorer OL2 - Yorkshire Dales South/West

ACCESS Start from Elm Tree Square at the top of the village. Car park a few yards along the street. Served by bus from Skipton.
•OPEN ACCESS: see page 6.

> A superb walk over fascinating and colourful moorland

      Partly inside the National Park boundary, Embsay is a thriving and sizeable village sandwiched between Skipton town and the open moors. It was here that the Augustinians began work before opting for the Wharfe's banks instead to found Bolton Priory. Embsay is home to the preserved Embsay & Bolton Abbey Steam Railway, painstakingly restored all the way to Bolton Abbey station, offering a return trip of some 12 miles on the former Skipton-Ilkley line: it has refreshments and giftshop. There are two pubs, the Cavendish and the Elm Tree, and a Post office/shop.

      Leave the village by a kissing-gate at the back of the car park, and bear left to a stile at the top corner of the field. The slender path slants up again, then crosses the fields behind the school and houses. *Up to the right the bracken-clad flanks of Embsay Crag beckon, with Crookrise Crag set back to its left. Both these eminences are visited on WALK 24.* Approaching a lone house on the right, a stile will be found down in the corner. This admits to a back road opposite an attractive millpond popular with ducks and swans. *The distinguished house overlooking it just along to the left bears a 1665 datestone (see page 95).*

Turn right on the lane rising to the grassy dam of Embsay Reservoir. *A shame the waterworks buildings couldn't be better masked, but the moorland flanks above set the pulse racing. Pendle Hill is an early part of the view far to the south-west.* The rocky outcrops of Deer Gallows are distinctive on the skyline ahead: it is useful to pick out the line of a path slanting up that way, soon it will be underfoot. *Embsay Crag is over to the right, with the start of Crookrise Crag to the left.* Bear left to the reservoir

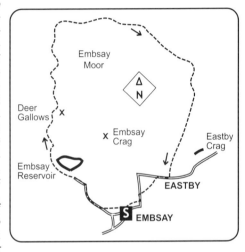

corner and along the stony track alongside. When the wall parts company take a stile in the fence to gain the foot of the open moor.

A level green path heads away above the wall. Within yards, after crossing a marshy streamlet, turn unconvincingly up through the bracken, with a small marsh on your left. Very quickly entering a grassy clearing, cross another streamlet, slant a little more and a clearer path forms in denser bracken. Not too much higher is a distinct fork in a smaller clearing. The left branch climbs more directly, while the nicer right branch slants more, past a small boulder. *The surroundings are magnificent: Embsay Crag across to the right, and a bird's-eye view of the reservoir. Look back over Skipton to the Aire Valley backed by the Pennine watershed, re-forming after the major interruption of the Aire Gap.*

On swinging back left a broader sunken way is joined, and this leads further up to a bend where the earlier left branch is just three strides away. If not locating this, remain on your right branch soon rising more narrowly but still clear to arrive at a cairn at the start of a broad grassy clearing. The rocks of Deer Gallows make an inviting landmark now just a short way above. Go left a few steps to a small isolated rock, then a trod slants left through less dense bracken to cross to finally rejoin the left branch. This now makes a grand gentle ascent through diminishing bracken, as heather starts to make an appearance. The way virtually levels out amid a few reeds, and runs on to a pair of stone piles. Deer Gallows is just across to the right beyond a line of grouse butts. On the open top, a trod is met at right angles in the moor grass. *One could keep straight on over this, but would sacrifice Deer Gallows.*

The detour to Deer Gallows is a five-minute level march. *This superb spot is popular with climbers, the main cliff face of archetypal millstone grit tilted gently back and riven by great rounded gashes. Facing it just across a green floor is the added attraction of a rock tower, composed of exactly the same layout, block upon block.*

Deer Gallows

From the crest of the main stones return to the path and resume, now almost level, with a marshy tract on your left. A firmer grassy track quickly takes over, and almost as quickly transforms into a firm Landrover track just yards short of the brow of East Harts Hill. *This brings a magnificent prospect of the interior of the moor. Cracoe Fell's obelisk sits on the skyline ahead. In late summer, these rolling heather seas are positively outstanding. Look back to a sweeping panorama of the South Pennines, Pendle Hill, Longridge Fell and the Bowland moors, the Malhamdale hills, mighty Ingleborough and Fountains Fell.*

Simply remain on this track to commence a long, steady descent to Waterfall Gill and rising to a pair of thatched shooters' cabins. *These come as a surprise, traditionally constructed of local stone with a bilberry thatch-like topping!* Keep straight up to absorb a bridleway coming in. *This historic route was immortalised by Wordsworth in his poem 'The White Doe of Rylstone'. The story of the ill-fated Nortons of Rylstone tells of a widow undertaking the trek over the moor to visit her husband's grave at Bolton Priory: the pet deer that accompanied her continued the journeys even after her death.* Remain on the shooters' track which runs eastwards, encouraging long strides on a grand, gently rising course.

A guidepost close by scattered rocks on the track summit at some 1410ft/430m sends a thin trod away bound for Embsay: ignore this and keep straight on. *A new view is revealed as Simon's Seat and Barden Fell appear across delectable Wharfedale.* Just yards beyond, ignore a track heading off left to Upper Barden Reservoir, which appears at this point. *Lower Barden Reservoir soon comes into the scene down below, and more of Wharfedale is revealed.* The track spends some time running an almost level promenade to enjoy this glorious prospect with a growing sense that this is to be a descent into Wharfedale.

About a mile beyond the high point the track descends more markedly, to find a distinct and inviting green path doubling back left: at this point take instead a slim but clear trod to the right through heather and bilberry. It leads to the breached dam of an old reservoir at Hutchen Gill Head, then straight on a short-lived trough to a stone shooters' cabin. Here another track arrives, climbing from the one you recently left. Just beyond is an inferior cabin, but your track turns up to the right just before it. Keep left at an early fork to run along to the first of a row of butts. *Embsay Crag by now presents a stunning profile with Pendle Hill beyond.* Follow the butts on a fainter path, gradually losing both height and heather en route to the last one. *Over to the right, Embsay Crag is seen at its finest angle. Ahead is Skipton Moor, high above a big quarry, with the Rombalds Moor skyline back to its left. With green fields ahead, it becomes clear you are running out of moor!*

At the final butt a thin trod bears gently left down to a ladder-stile at Eastby Gate. Pass through some pens and down the wallside track through a couple of ladder-stiles to the edge of Heugh Gill. *A nice moment is gained above the side gill ahead, with Embsay Crag's profile now reaching exalted status.* The track descends above it to become deeply ensconced in a hollowed, leafy way, before emerging into a yard at Eastby and down onto the road. *This tiny farming village is strung along the road from Embsay over the moor to Barden, and has a pub, the Masons Arms.*

Turn right, leaving the village and then leaving the road at a path on the left. There is a certain quaintness to the tarmac strip of path, not more than a foot wide as it runs through the fields to Embsay's church of St Mary the Virgin. At the road, follow it left past the church, and take a stile on the right. Head across to a corner stile, from where an enclosed path runs to emerge into the field above Embsay's car park.

At the heart of Embsay: the Elm Tree Inn

CROOKRISE CRAG

START *Embsay   Grid ref. SD 998544*

DISTANCE *5³4 miles (9km)*

ORDNANCE SURVEY MAPS
1:50,000
Landranger 103 - Blackburn & Burnley
Landranger 104 - Leeds, Bradford & Harrogate
1:25,000
Explorer OL2 - Yorkshire Dales South/West

ACCESS *Start from Embsay Reservoir, reached by Pasture Road off Elm Tree Square at the top of the village. Water company car park. Embsay is served by bus from Skipton.* •*OPEN ACCESS: see page 6.*

> *Exhilarating walking linking inspiring natural landmarks on the rolling moors above Embsay*

Embsay Reservoir has a fine setting under Embsay Crag and the moor itself. Its facilities are shared by sailing and angling clubs. From the car park head left along the stony track outside the reservoir, past the sailing club to the far end. Here its confining walls break away and a stile gives access to the open moor. Turn left onto a path beginning an immediate climb through bracken, soon accompanying the wall on the left. Remaining near the wall, the path further improves and passes through characterful boulder scenery before levelling out. Soon the first of several stiles in the wall is reached: use it to attain the top of the cliffs of Crookrise Crag, a breathtaking moment.

The panorama stretches from the Aire Valley to the South Pennine moors and round to the familiar outline of Pendle Hill. Beyond are Longridge and Grindleton Fells and the massive

Bowland moors skyline, then the Malhamdale hills of Kirkby Fell and Pikedaw intervene with Ingleborough's flat top peeking over the latter. Flasby Fell's little peaks are directly in front, while the higher reaches of the Dales fill in the rest of the scene to the north. Now confined in the narrow space between the steep drop and the wall, continue northward on a thin path straight towards the white trig. point which soon comes into sight.

At 1361ft/415m, this is Crookrise Crag Top. *The expanse of heather-clad upland known as Barden Moor comes to an abrupt halt at many places around its rim, but nowhere as dramatic as Crookrise, where a long line of crags fall steeply to an unnatural green carpet of conifers. In between are a tumble of mill-stone grit boulders, and this whole scene forms a splendid sight for travellers on the road between Skipton and Rylstone. The crags are substantial enough* to offer a varied range of challenges for rock climbers.

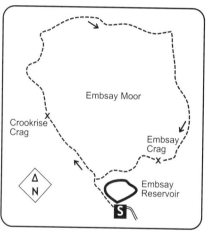

After surveying the extensive panorama a stile returns you to the moorland side of the wall, to continue northward over small boulders. Path and wall remain close as denser bracken takes over, dropping to the massive blocky boulders of Hellifield Crags. As the trees over the wall end, the path runs a level course to arrive above a steep plunge to Waterfall Gill, a splendid moment. The drop is largely avoided as the path slants down to the right beneath the more extensive lower boulders of Hellifield Crags. *Just before reaching the beck a fine waterfall should be seen from above.* Once across, the path climbs steeply through bracken by an initially crumbling wall. The gradient soon eases and the wall leads to a gate where the Rylstone-Bolton Abbey track passes through.

Crookrise Crag

Your route takes advantage of this way, and turns to the right along it. *This historic route was immortalised by Wordsworth in his poem 'The White Doe of Rylstone'. The story of the ill-fated Nortons of Rylstone tells of a widow undertaking the trek over the moor to visit her husband's grave at Bolton Priory: the pet deer that accompanied her continued the journeys even after her death. Followed onto the heart of the moor, the distinct path has seen much restoration at a normally boggy section by the laying of a durable surface.* This remains your way for almost a mile and a half. Further on you merge into a more traditional shooters' track coming up from a pair of thatched cabins, and continue to stride out in grand style, rising ever gradually to the brow of the hill.

Here close by scattered rocks on the track summit at some 1410ft/430m a guidepost sends a thin, almost dead-flat trod off to the right. *As the ground opens up ahead the view sweeps from Simon's Seat around to Beamsley Beacon, with Chelker's reservoir and windfarm prominent and Ilkley sat beneath Rombalds Moor.* As the path winds down through heather Embsay Crag gains in stature. As the path drops further to enter bracken a distinct path forks right, rising to bring Embsay Crag back into the scene, a striking profile now just ahead. A super path runs on through heather towards it, utilising this neck of connecting land to run to a short pull onto the crest, a location that is not in doubt.

Jutting from the vast moorland, the modest 1217ft/371m Embsay Crag is a notable landmark in the Skipton area. Dense bracken cloaks the lower slopes, while a delectable carpet of heather crowns the top. The crag is actually a tumble of boulders heaped together in wonderful chaos on the southern slopes of the hill. This is gritstone country at its best, and the highest rocks are the perfect location for a long lazy break on a hot summer's day, with the reservoir shimmering far below your airy vantage point.

The main path can clearly be seen descending the steepest section directly below, and is well blazed through the bracken beyond. A friendlier way down, however, is to follow another clear path along the brink of the rocks across to the right: this descends in similar fashion to your route of ascent, and after exchanging the heather for dense bracken descends a little more steeply and swings left along it to meet the main path down from the crag. This leads unerringly down to a footbridge by the head of the reservoir. Across it ascend briefly, and the path bears right to join a broader green one which leads to the stile back off the moor.

Embsay Crag from the reservoir

WALK LOG

WALK	DATE	NOTES
1		
2		
3		
4		
5		
6		
7		
8		
9		
10		
11		
12		
13		
14		
15		
16		
17		
18		
19		
20		
21		
22		
23		
24		

USEFUL ADDRESSES

Ramblers' Association
2nd Floor, Camelford House, 87-89 Albert Embankment, London SE1 7BR
• 020-7339 8500

Yorkshire Dales National Park
Colvend, Hebden Road, Grassington, Skipton BD23 5LB
• 01756-752748   www.yorkshiredales.org.uk

Yorkshire Tourist Board
312 Tadcaster Road, York YO2 2HF • 01904-707961

Yorkshire Dales Society
Town Hall, Cheapside, Settle BD24 9EJ • 01729-825600

Tourist Information/National Park Centres
Malham • 01729-830363

35 Coach Street **Skipton** • 01756-792809

Town Hall, Cheapside **Settle** • 01729-825192

Hebden Road **Grassington** • 01756-752774

Open Access
Helpline • 0845-100 3298 *or* www.countrysideaccess.gov.uk

Bolton Abbey estate office • 01756-710227

Public Transport Information
Traveline
• 0870 608 2608
National Rail Enquiries
• 08457-484950

At the millponds, Embsay

INDEX
walk number refers

Aire Head Springs 4
Aire, River 4,12,13,16,18
Airton 12,13
Attermire Scar 7

Bank Newton 18
Bell Busk 13,16
Bordley 10,20
Boss Moor 20

Calton 11
Calton Moor 11
Coniston Cold 16
Cracoe 21
Cracoe Fell 21
Crookrise Crag 24

Darnbrook 9
Deer Gallows 23

Eastby 23
East Marton 18
Embsay 23
Embsay Crag 24
Embsay Moor 23,24
Embsay Reservoir 23,24
Eshton 17

Flasby 22
Flasby Fell 22
Fountains Fell 6
Friars Head 18,19

Gargrave 16,17,18
Gordale Scar 1,5,8

Hanlith 5,12

Haw Crag 13
Hetton 22

Janet's Foss 1,5,8

Kirkby Fell 2
Kirkby Malham 4,12
Knowe Fell 6

Langber Lane 14,15
Leeds-Liverpool Canal 16,17,18
Long Preston 15

Malham 1,2,3,4,5
Malham Cove 1,3
Malham Tarn 6,8,9
Mastiles Lane 10

Otterburn 14

Pikedaw 2

Rough Haw 22
Rylstone 21,22
Rylstone Fell 21

Sharp Haw 22
Stockdale 7

Victoria Cave 7

Warrendale Knotts 7
Water Sinks 3,7
Watlowes 3
Weets Top 5
Winterburn 19
Winterburn Reservoir 11,19